T0194306

NAKED TREES

PAUL ZEPPELIN

NAKED TREES

iUniverse books may be ordered through booksellers or by contacting:

iUniverse
1663 Liberty Drive
Bloomington, IN 47403
www.iuniverse.com
1-800-Authors (1-800-288-4677)

ISBN: 978-1-6632-0488-2 (sc)
ISBN: 978-1-6632-0489-9 (e)

Library of Congress Control Number: 2020912941

Print information available on the last page.

iUniverse rev. date: 07/15/2020

Preface

The readers will certainly enjoy this new collection of poetry as they and I enjoyed the earlier collection of Paul Zeppelin's poetry, *Shattered Silence.* Once again, he gives us a vibrant, imaginary world of strong emotions, allegories, love, courage, dreams, betrayal, deep philosophy, and at times, despair. However, his poetry is pierced with vivid rays of hope.

His intriguing language is a remarkable combination of country limerick and a traditional elegance of classicism.

Judith Parrish Broadbent
Author of *Golden Days:*
Stories and Poems from the
Middle South and Beyond.

Epigraph

The moon was hiding
In the clouds,
My soul performed
A self-discovery striptease,
It shed its ancient shrouds
In front of the
Laughing naked trees.

Contents

A Cornerstone of Life

I am searching like a scout bee
A haven for a sacred hive,
A harbor for a cornerstone of life;
The heavens whisper, "Let it be."

Victorious in war, I lost my peace:
My sword is resting in the sheath;
I walk between the naked trees,
And wear a thorny crown-wreath.

There's nothing left to prove,
My worn-out mind and heart
Run over the parting groove
Of lies in life and truths in art.

The truth unfortunately fails
As dough without leaven,
Only one guy and no one else
Dwells in the promised Heaven.

He took away my sins and fear,
But yet nobody could explain
Why I am so lonely down here
And no one lulls my endless pain.

The Darkest Corner

Across the silence of a deserted field.
We write the signs: stop, walk or yield.

Today, my angel said
Digesting quesadilla,
"Live like a newlywed".
I loved the great idea.

The darkest corner of my troubled soul
Devours virtuous ideas by its Black Hole.
Across a silence of a forsaken battlefield
We write the signs: "stop, walk and yield".

A rival of my enemy,
Is not necessarily a friend;
The laws are written not for me,
I am a rebel; I hold the devil's hand:
My life is just a constant intercourse
With our lethargic, sleepy world,
While all the lovely whores
Work on the lower Broad.

I am not a pervert,
My fattest chances
Entirely introverted,
I like exotic dancers.

Death penalty doesn't exist,
I sip the venom of my priest.

The Dawn's Amazing Light

Foretellers never saw my eyes,
Foretellers never knew my soul,
They arrogantly tossed the dice
And watched the numbers roll.

Springs vindicate my wait,
Weeds find their own way
To Granny's garden gate.
Long live the rite of May.

The image of renewal looms
Over routinely sunny springs,
Flaunting its cherry blooms
Between the rainy strings.

I stroked a miserable sound
Then laid my old guitar aside,
I am ready for a vodka round,
Spring takes me for a jolly ride.

Spring reaches for my hand
And ushers me into the ice,
In vain, I try to recognize
The Promised Land.
Only the dead may see the
Paradise.

I walk beyond the sunny slopes,
Across the harbor of my hopes,
I am ready for my reckless flight
Into the dawn's amazing light.

The Daisies in Your Hair

The mighty branches swing
Under the frightened moon,
The hiding birds don't sing,
The cats and horses swoon.

I am drinking in the den,
The dog sits at my feet,
A noiseless ceiling fan
Caresses summer heat.

A storm without thunders,
A chess without blunders,
A dirty dog without a smell;
Am I in heaven or in hell?

A sterile life is not for me,
I drown in this glue,
I want to run away, to flee,
But not without you.

My eyes are sadly dry:
My tears were sown,
I reaped the silent cry
Of boredom in my soul.

I carved my verse
Like morning dew
Of a sincere remorse;
I gave my heart to you.

The daisies in your hair,
The flowers of our affair,
Your tender loving smile
Rock in my luscious wine.

Your tears were sown,
I only reaped the cry,
Our hearts have flown
Into the anxious sky.

The Ditch of Old Affairs

My shark-finned bail
Picks up some speed,
Flees from the prying
Cells and corridors of jail;
Conceals forever crying
Eyes of those who bleed,
Of those who're still dying,
Of those who'll tell the tale
About a haven of the freed,
About lullabies of waves
That rock the fallen leaves;
About our fallen braves
Between the naked trees.

I lived my tabulated days:
No creativity, no courage
In silence and nightmares;
I slid into a dreary place
For my lackluster voyage,
Into the ditch of old affairs;
Its blue lethargic glow
Derailed me overboard;
I gratefully enjoy the flow
Of nature's infinite accord.

I am just a pawn,
I walk the ground,
Yet leave no trace.
I see the rays of dawn,
I hear the jovial sound,
Of the "Amazing Grace".

The Crescent in the Starry Sky

I am a stranger in this world,
The crescent in the starry sky
Hangs as the Damocles sword
Above my neck. I wonder why?

I stand my ground,
I am a young recruit,
I am red, white and blue,
I am in a hot pursuit;
Here is your only clue:
I am a hungry hound,
Don't paddle my canoe,
I am the crescent bound.

Life is the greatest book,
I slowly read, delay the end,
Like a wild marlin on the hook,
I jump, I stretch and bend,
The line is a mile long,
Am I that strong?
I am not the sharpest pencil
In the box,
I am not crazy like a fox.
There is my life at stake,
Have merci for God's sake.

The Crumbling Citadel

In search of laurels for my wins
I sailed into a harbor of my sins;
I saw the crumbling citadel,
I heard the silence of its bell.

I saw the ends of endless ropes,
The final bastions of darkness,
And yet I saw the rays of hopes
Cancelled among the heartless.

Bombarding cancerous rumors
Will not annihilate their distance,
Will only harden vicious tumors
Of scuttlebutts and coexistence.

I am fighting bottles of my life,
Stirring the sediments of strife;
And as a symbolic self-discovery,
I will be revived after the Calvary.

I will destroy the evil spell,
I am sworn to win this war;
We will not meet in Hell,
The heaven awaits--I soar.

Without My Footprints

That morning was tongue-tied,
Only a tormented evening cried:
A poet, their beloved boy
Was killed in the devil's ploy.
The skies turned gray
Above advancing flames
Lengthwise eternal runway
For worthy yet unknown names.

I learned to walk without leaving
My footprints…

My life is like a book
Without a preface and epilogue
But with the seven empty pages
For nonexistent seven mortal sins;
A dire creation of a virginal infinity,
But with a printed hefty price
On its glossy cover…

Only the birds sing free,
They live in bliss; they live in glee.
They sing for the humble
And for the mighty of the world;
I've heard the sacramental word.
They sing for me.

I burned my cherished strophes,
My foes won't get their trophies:
My footprints on the eternal strife
Of death and life.

My Vision Faints

Today, I wear a suit,
Tomorrow,
I'll be wrapped in shrouds,
Today, I walk barefoot,
Tomorrow,
I'll soar above the clouds.

The candles mourn my sin,
I wipe their tears of paraffin,
I dared to raise my mighty sword,
I dared to stand against the Lord.

This time he ruined peace,
This time he took our best,
But, damn it, why?
My brothers longed for bliss,
My brothers simply guessed,
His order was to fight and die.

The Arlington's saluted,
The navy banners swayed,
Wars killed and looted,
The youth was calmly laid.

My weary memory attains
Sweet images of vanished friends,
But suddenly my vision faints,
Only my trembling hands,
Only the teardrops on my cheeks,
Only the gleaming flames,
Only the candles' brittle wicks
Remember their forgotten names.

Nirvana

My spacious glassy hall
Lit by the gleaming moon,
The Mona Lisa on the wall,
Forged by a local goon.

A glass of a red wine
Between two candles,
The night erased a line
Between two genders…
.
A tenor sings a serenade
To his beloved concubine,
The gloomy shadows fade,
I sip my luscious wine.

Nirvana covers me with silk,
Pure as my mother's lullaby,
Even the stars begin to blink,
I whisper to my worries, bye.

While Empty Pages Wait

I live, I cannot stop, I cannot fall asleep,
I have to be on top while others weep,
I am a shark circling the bogus bait,
I swim while empty pages wait.

The tears of rain fall on my face,
I hug my flesh, a very sad embrace,
Chained to my muse, my lifelong love,
To wisdom we both use fits like a glove.

We had to cross the bridge,
Being the prisoners of time;
Our hearts are in the fridge,
Cold is a perfect paradigm.

I must unlock the door,
And let my talents flee,
Into the joy galore
To share my glee.

My masquerade is blown,
I am back to vicious races,
I throw everything I own
Into my opponents faces.

I live, I cannot stop,
I have to be on top.

Nostalgic Tears of Rage

They look at me
Through empty eyes
Of broken windows;
They reprimand me
For the hidden cries
Of mourning widows.

Abandoned homes,
Forbidden streets,
Imagination roams
Amid the bits of wits.

Nostalgic tears of rage
Confront me in the street,
Today, I am a silver sage,
I still don't miss the beat,
Forgiveness in my heart
Lives as the grace of art.

I am never tired
Of being called a hero
By my devoted friends.
I am alive, I am admired;
I looked into the mirror,
And washed my hands.

Ode to René Magritte Start Here

Surrealistic fairytales
Carved by René Magritte:
Unknown, hidden trails,
Suspended apple's treat,
A hat of Chaplin's plays,
Bare windows brightly lit,
A train over two shiny rails,
Two parallels forever meet.

Defensive pessimism,
Rose-colored glasses,
New genius, another ism,
A puzzle for the masses.

The mediocre and obtuse
Take solace in your sins:
Magritte will burn the fuse,
Irrationality as always wins.

No one commits all seven.
He told the sleepy dawn,
"Hello, is there someone
Who dwells in heaven?"
Nobody ever heard the bell,
Nobody lives in bliss or hell.

Two shiny parallels,
One vicious treat,
Two stubborn rails,
One path into defeat.

Our entertainment vanished
In silent gestures of a mime,
Another genius was punished
For being far ahead of time.

Sunset Will Fade

A red sunset will fade
Like a bullfighter's rag,
I will unfurl from shade,
The rebels' tattered flag.

The iron horse moves us
Ahead,
Some never get their silver
Spoon,
Some never get their daily
Bread,
Some get too much
And swoon.

I am getting used to life
Along the slowest lane,
I lost my home and wife,
She let me keep my brain.

One sparrow doesn't make
The spring,
One vendor doesn't make
The fair,
Although, even the mute
Will sing,
When life is awfully hard
To bear.

Life brings me up to speed,
It offers gluttony and greed,
My aspirations will not drain,
I will not lose my pride in pain.

When facts get squeezed
Before my staggered eyes,
Life shows a political striptease,
I have to watch its barefaced lies.

Red-haired Van Gogh

Red-haired Van Gogh
Foresaw a magic play:
Stars twirled the tango
Across the Milky Way.

Sunflowers and trees
Stood heavyhearted
Beneath the dancing stars;
The moon abruptly started
To cast the shadows' scars.

The diamonds of tears
Ran down as the years
While life hung as a yoke;
He could no longer bear
His overwhelming fears
Over the rim of his despair.

He'll hold his heart in hand,
He'll start his last romance,
He'll leave this cruel land,
He'll begin his final dance,
He'll stop his earthly farce,
He'll tango with the stars.

Salome Wants to Dance

Salome wants to dance,
She takes her chance.
King Herod grants a wish,
Ballet of the seven veils,
John's head is on the dish,
Poor Baptist. Evil never fails.

Why can't we forgive?
Because we learned to take,
We never learned to give.
We fight for the fight's sake,
We never turn another cheek,
We think it makes us weak.

The flow of dark days,
The stream of salty tears;
Our wisdom whispers,
"An eye for an eye,
Forget forgiveness,
It's hard, don't try".

Our hearts are hardened,
We are estranged,
Our souls are pardoned,
Our wills are drenched;
Our seven sins have gone,
Yet, we forgave no one,

Above the golden leaves,
I heard the angel's word,
"No one forgives,
Only the Lord."

Seagulls are Praying for Your Soul

Tough life has turned me on a dime,
I didn't do the crime, I do the time,
The scary dimness tightly wraps me,
I meet the good, the bad, and ugly.

I see the image of my friend,
I hung his photo on the wall,
He flies above our sinful land,
He is beyond the curtain call.

I used to like a young sunrise,
Today, I watch a fiery sunset:
My buddy paid a heavy price.
Farewell didn't erase my debt.

Death came barefaced, no mask,
I am sipping brandy from my flask;
My bosom friend, you hear the toll,
Seagulls are praying for your soul.

Your name is chiseled in my heart,
A fine calligraphy is a forgotten art.
We were together in our gory fights,
We are together in my joyless nights.

Another Tattered Page

Her eyes looked like the fallen sky,
She was not ready for a laughter,
She was inclined to whine or cry.
I heard her soul tearing sighs,
She grieved the morning after.

Another tattered page
Flew out of my book
Into a golden cage,
Into a cozy nook.

All my imprisoned verses,
Inspired by a sad-eyed muse,
Sang under the yoke of curses
Their tearful eternal blues...

Too much, too soon,
Too few, too late;
I sold my silver spoon,
I threw away my fate.

My inquisition failed,
Life didn't share its files,
But I am a hawk, red tailed,
I see the insincerity of smiles.

Even the trusting plants inhale
Our poisoned breaths;
We know a few myths we trail,
We trust in lives past our deaths.

They Wake Desires

I edged ahead of motivated hordes,
A threaded needle hems my words.

I crave, but cannot find
The rivers of new tears,
All problems are behind,
And only my future veers.

I love this time, I see no threat,
Dawn and sunrise, dusk and sunset.
Under the guise of playful days
A loud breeze and silence of malaise.

Across my dreamy walk
The raindrops swiftly fall
And pierce my tatty cloak,
And occupy my thirsty soul

I hear tormented strings
A winter plays its old guitars,
I spot the tunes of springs
Stubbornly rising to the stars.

The sparkly stars tease nightly skies,
While freeze is far, they wake desires.

The dazzling flowerbeds
Under the beams of grace,
Extend their hungry hands,
And shiver in my hot embrace.

Numbing Darkness

Man shall not live by bread alone,
But by the words leaving his breath,
I wish the epitaph on my tombstone
Will say: "He danced himself to death."

The nights were always young
On naughty Rue de St. Denis.
She let me use my native tongue,
It was my first; it was my glee.

I couldn't see her beauty in the dark,
Her very pleasing voice said "Anna."
Her lovely name was like a spark
Igniting my anticipation of nirvana.

Under the freezing strings of rain,
I heard a brittle tune of cracking ice:
Spring's requiem for melting freeze,
Under the shadow of a flying crane,
Returning to this earthly paradise
After the winter's voyage overseas.

I sailed eternal seas of ignorance,
Between the scattered isles of reason,
I passed them in a numbing darkness,
Remaining rather bold and vigorous,
Knowing this world as a twilight zone,
Obscurely weird but seldom heartless.

I held my unassailable belief
In a great goodness of a thief,
That begged the rite of dawn
To save a life, I tried to pawn.

A healthy measure of my nihilism
Wrapped in a quilt of sewn wishes,
Allows me, beyond my skepticism,
To see the Holy grail in dirty dishes.

Calembour

To be in a QUEUE or in LINE,
Who cares; they both are fine.
You mumble AIN'T or AREN'T,
It is your tongue, don't harm it.

You use a PLOW or a PLOUGH,
I am as quiet as a well-fed cow,
But if you call my DOG a DAWG,
Then you are just a real HAWG.

I bet you say a loud GOOD
Instead of a proper WELL,
I checked under your hood,
An absolutely empty shell.

I almost forgot your ME and I.
Please, try to learn. Goodbye.

She Always Knew It All

We walked, I held her hand,
My date was a divine allure,
Her body was a fertile land,
So loving, young and pure.

She picked an autumn leaf,
She hid it from the breeze,
Her face was veiled in grief,
She couldn't stop the freeze.

I used to be a hollow toll,
I learned from her this all:
A quilt of sheepish clouds,
A waltz for swirling leaves,
A masked ball of the saints,
A bedspread of the doubts,
A graveyard for the thieves,
A stockroom for complaints.

She lulled the pains of life
And problems of the world,
She knew the sacred word,
She was my gorgeous wife.

She Airs her Balanced Thoughts

She used to introduce a ban
On innocence to our schools,
These days, she is a captain,
Of the renowned ship of fools.

She pulls her thoughts
Into my solitary bed
About missing shots,
About baking bread,
About noisy silence,
About empty science,
About our face value,
About humans' bayou.

My wheels don't roll,
She is obsessed,
The leaves don't fall,
She is depressed
By carrots and the sticks
Of good, ole' dirty politics:
Praying away the rain
To real meteorology
Is like a passing train
To modern gynecology.

She is our Lady Justice with a grin,
She grants forgiveness to a sin,
She firmly holds a sword in hands,
She threatens us with reprimands,
She is forever thoughtfully blind,
She trusts her evenhanded mind.

She airs her well-adjusted thoughts
She loads our heads as empty pots.

Scorecards of Life

I watch the silhouettes
Of aiming faceless guards,
These merciless judges
Of my life's scorecards.

The saints can rise from hell to Eden,
They can afford the cost of freedom,
I have not ever seen that many zeros,
But saw my loneliness in dusty mirrors.

My life was bent like a horseshoe
I pitched it toward the pit of death.
It landed in a honeydew,
Pure as a baby's breath.

Life left a few footprints
On quiet memoirs of times.
A striking lightness brought its Prince
Rejecting punishments for our crimes.

Hegelian approach to dialectics:
Reality of contradictions
And synthesis of an unknown
Mixed intellectual anorectics
Without justified convictions
With vanities and egos overblown.

Lackluster quilt of ten commandments
Prevents reality from reenactments
Of naughty sins in my atrocious past,
I am reliving my seclusion of an outcast.

I am in front of faceless aiming guards,
The final readers of my life's scorecards

She Sought to Love Me Free

Why do I speak new tongues
In my astounding nightmares?
I'd rather listen to the songs
Of sentimental nightingales.

I used to be too bold
To have a quiet life,
Today, I am too old
To have a loving wife.

She sought to love me free,
I didn't trust, I paid,
I squandered precious glee,
I could no longer wait.

I am a captive of gray clouds,
I am swimming in the smoke,
I am making useless rounds,
I lose myself in every stroke.

I hear the roar of forest fires
Deep in my life's quagmires,
The thirsty oceans lure me
Beneath the ripples' filigree.

I am a good guy with a twist:
The future is quite bright,
I have to wear my shades
To see the wrong from right.
I guess, I am not a pessimist:
Without puzzles and charades,
I try to figure out what's in my cards,
Do I deserve the whole nine yards?

The Sun Continuously Rises

I came too late,
I was a dollar short,
And didn't buy a ticket,
My ship has left the port,
It was my unforgiving fate,
At times, murky and wicked.

The precious ambers
Of the autumn leaves,
Fall like nostalgic embers
Of life that quietly retrieves.

I came from work too late,
The ball was in my court;
It was my bitter fate,
My ship has left the port.

Even the dead cats bounce,
Even dried branches sway,
And tenderly pronounce,
"Long live another day!"

My intuition said
"The king is dead,
A swan must sing,
Long live the king!"

Our paradise disguises
In a good life without limits;
The sun continuously rises,
And soars into the zenith.

Another afternoon,
No clouds in the sky;
I miss my mother's lullaby
About kindness of the moon.

Spring Fiddles

Pine needles,
Thorny scent,
Spring fiddles,
Winter went.

The headless necks,
The stumps of trees,
The victims of the ax,
The guards of freeze.

The early yellow flowers
Poke through the snow,
A very few warm hours
And streams will flow.

New spring, new strife,
The first warm breeze
Brings death and life,
Brings war and peace.

Old winter hit the skids,
Her frigid reign is over:
Spring places hefty bids
On a four-petaled clover.

Silence of Pain or Pain of Silence

There are too many things
That can't be seen or heard:
Silence of pain or pain of silence,
The silence of my broken heart,
The pain of your irrational defiance.
The silence of a violin without strings,
The pain of a coldblooded firebird,
Unanswered loves that died in vain,
My melancholy on a menu a la cart.

My days are breeding grounds,
Under the noiseless clouds,
No matter shine or rain.
Why can't I bear my pain?
My life has almost passed,
Time couldn't melt the ice,
I veered from blast to blast,
Collecting pains for paradise.

There are no metronomes of time,
The silent pains don't cry or sing,
They carry their predestined cross
Only a passionate but silent mime
Reminds me of a flying albatross
With a broken wing.

The dogs and seagulls face the wind,
The humans turn their backs or pray,
The birds and dogs have never sinned,
Or maybe angels looked the other way.
We can't survive without sins
The truce is largely holding
Between the friends and fiends,
Our banners are unfolding

And trembling in the winds.
There are some pains in every story,
I recognize and feel them all;
I tried to give them Heaven's glory,
And placed them in the Wailing Wall.

The Sun Still Burns

You flaunt a knotted smile
Amid the cries and laughs,
I am a mediator in the trial
Among two fighting halves.

Don't close your eyes,
Don't close your ears,
Don't cease your life;
I'll hear your cries,
I'll wipe your tears,
You are my wife.

The sun still burns,
But doesn't warm
What's left of me;
I missed my turns,
I missed the storm,
I am a lifeless tree.

There is no night,
There is no day,
Only the winless fight,
Only the endless play.

I tore and burned
The lifelong tape
Of our futile fight;
Sobriety adjourned
My devilish escape
Into the starry night.

Old-fashioned Urge

My habits' old graveyards
Locked all the exit doors;
I am alive: my credit cards
Accepted by the whores.

My strong desire to reemerge
And crush newly acquired lies;
Stirred the old-fashioned urge
To see reality with my own eyes.

I am taking dusty roads back,
Reentering my childhood fever,
I stroll a single-minded track
Among the takers, I am a giver.

Surrounded with people,
Being a harbor for a tease,
I am rolling like a lazy ripple,
Not to contest, but please;
Never the last,
Never the first,
Under a chronic overcast
Of my pathetic endless thirst.

I realized, when reasons sleep
The fallen angel prospers,
Nevertheless, my brainy punches
Just mirror my liturgic conscience
As long as our preachers weep.
I still am reading our four gospels.

I buried years I wastefully spent,
I am out of that never-ending drain,
But wonder what my angels meant
When they gave me such a nosy brain.

The Star of David

Don't dare, Raise voice
Rake flock Don't mock
It is unfair, Make noise,
Knock lock. Crash rock

Find gist, Ding-dong, Move Back

But then, Ping pong, Go West
Go East, Dong-ding, And wreck
My man. Pong ping. Your nest.

Ding-dong See South, Hit strong
Bum, bum, Miles long. Bite tongue,
King Kong Loud mouth, Start clock,
Dumb, dumb. Gray thong. Turn block.

Wet mop, Right song,
Go North, Sing wrong,
Flip-flop Big throng,
It's worth. Hong Kong.

Young boys,
Brave ducks,
Huge choice,
Green bucks.

I've shown to the world
My golden paper gown,
Just take my final word,
As king, I wear a crown.

Over the Killing Fields

No one can catch
The falling stars,
No one can heal
The wartime scars
From shattered dreams,
From petrifying screams,
From running silhouettes
Of horrifying fatal threats.

Our mothers' tears
Of ceaseless hours
Brought lavish yields
Of gorgeous flowers
Over the killing fields
Into eternity of years.

We are back home,
A timely metronome,
The war's heartbeat,
An unexpected treat
Was sent to us from
Battlefields of victory
And valleys of defeat.

We've grown in the shadows
Cast by the dishonest claims;
Only the fallen angel knows
The rules of modern games.

We slid into the hell,
The fiends already left,
The sinners restfully dwell,
In our world that is so deft.

.

She

She is my younger friend:
The infancy of our alliance
Requires my tender hand
To curb her mild defiance.

A little shy before her teacher,
She is eighteen and stunning,
But I am not a pious preacher,
I am not a saint, I am cunning.

I am not a lettered man,
I have no time to waste:
I am a rooster, she's a hen,
She is the fruit I want to taste.

She is the magnet of my whims,
She is the object of my desire,
She is the zenith of my dreams,
She is Prometheus of my fire.

No one is wrong or right,
No one is a predator or prey:
All cats are gray at night,
Life is an all-you-can-eat buffet.

I am abstract,
I am divorced
From the reality:
My deck is stacked,
I am the worst
Of man's duality.

She Was a Real Gold

I went into a bar jam-packed
With intellectual diehards
Who tried to charm their luck,
Preoccupied by love and sex.
The others played some cards
Perhaps to lose or win a buck,
Or drumming out hollow texts.
I am just a clown on a trapeze
Right in the beams' crosshairs,
I watch her fabulous striptease
After my split-up's nightmares.
No one is acting apropos,
And I am ready to propose.

We were a drawbridge
Forever parted,
Two banks, one river
Cold as a fridge
And empty hearted,
Two takers, none a giver.

I read my poetry and prose
About heavens and the sun,
She dragged a handgun
From a leather sheathe,
The barrel zoomed and froze,
I didn't move, I didn't breathe,
My palms were sweaty cold;
She aimed at my forehead
And gently pulled the trigger:
She is alive, I am still dead.
She knew she was a real gold,
She thought, I was its digger.

Somebody Wrote in Error

A real life is death,
Somebody wrote in error.
A purity of baby's breath
Survives the reign of terror.

A real death is life,
The others wrote in error,
Ascent of one after a strife,
Nobody has repeated ever.

Life is a fight against the foes,
Death isn't a temporary sleep,
I wouldn't bring a water hose
To help a crocodile to weep.

I picture stories of Lot's wife,
She didn't turn to catch her
Breath,
Did she begin her endless
Death
Or simply ended her good
Life?

Only my granny knew the truth,
She taught me in my youth:
Life is a red banner for a bull,
Life is when a bill is paid in full;
Death is a rainbow to a blind,
Death is a talent left behind,
Death is a singing swan,
Life is a play that goes on:
Even the altars of despair
Are passionately worshiped,
The others think it is unfair

To pray without being whipped;
Bathwater never sees a baby,
Hard to believe but maybe.
Even a broken grandfather clock
Correctly works two times a day.
Only at night all cats seem gray.

Postmortem

I was against the wall of brine,
The fallen angel grasped his goal,
The surges rolled into my shrine,
The hurricane resided in my soul.

Eternal autumn:
The sea of rain,
I signed my own postmortem,
I rhymed my wounds and pain.

I used to pointlessly talk,
I used to wear the cloak,
I used to bleed,
I used to preach,
I used to lead
The blind into the ditch.

A squeaky deck was built
Along the harbor of my life,
I did not confess my guilt,
A rescue boat did not arrive.

I didn't turn my other cheek
I combed the mirror of a lake,
I found what I used to seek,
But it was just another fake.

I used to cherish
Life's every needed lesson;
The end was hellish,
I held my Smith & Wesson.

My Verses Die at Birth

My verse and I will meet
During the Judgment day;
We all will hear the beat,
And march on feet of clay.

Life silenced poesy in me,
My verses die at birth,
I turned into a fruitless tree,
Please, stop the Earth.

Good poets always imitate,
Great poets always steal,
The good will miss the gate,
The great will make a deal.

My verses are maligned,
Is it a crime I get away with?
My sentence will be signed,
The rhymes will fall beneath.

I hide a fragile humble hope
Among mirages of my youth,
I hold the Oscar's envelope,
Tonight, I will unveil the truth.

Our Short-lived Show

A few fragile snowflakes
Danced with the leaves
After the winter's blow,
Some flew above the lakes,
Some hovered off the cliffs
To wrap their lifelong show.

Spring left the womb,
Caressed by frosty air,
The early lilacs bloom
In their attractive flare.

The rivers stream away,
Unfurling waters' sway,
Old winter wants to cry
Beneath its mask of joy,
The birds relearn to fly,
The sun enjoys the ploy.

It was a sad romance,
Love came, but once,
We knew it;
We got it for a song,
We both were wrong,
We blew it.

We wrote a song of spring,
Yet none of us would sing;
We lost a link in our chain,
We couldn't bear the pain.

The judge was wisely briefed,
Nobody had the horn to blow,
Our love was harshly sieved,
We quit our short-lived show.

Our Whims

I see a falling star
And make a wish,
I hear a moving train
And make a wish;
I never send my hopes afar,
They may evaporate in vain.

Forget the plans of infancies,
Forget the sweetest dreams,
The morgues of fantasies
Dissect and tag our whims.

Don't hurry up to die,
Just change the gear,
And you will know why
Our fortunes veer.

No one should have the right
To start another bloody war,
No one would come to fight;
Give fragile peace a chance,
The bands will play and roar,
And we will learn to dance.

The lucky dice was thrown,
We wait for something new,
For something totally unknown,
Though it is only passing through.

My Autumns Were Your Springs

My autumns were your springs,
You let me spread my wings;
You were so innocently young,
You were a song but yet unsung.

The eagle of that love still flies,
High in the ocean of the skies.

We used to soar together,
Two restless, troubled souls,
Two birds; different feathers;
Two radicals, different goals.

We climbed too high,
We burned our wings;
The sun's apologetic sigh
Fell from its blinding rings.

Our happy careless hearts
Pierced by the cupid's darts,
Dismissed the warning bell,
We touched the sun. We fell.

The Sun Delays its Rounds

The tablecloth of clouds
Slid down from the skies,
The sun delays its rounds
Over our tears and cries.

The history exhumes
Our tarnished times
From dormant tombs,
The final judgment looms
Above unwritten rhymes
Still in the fertile wombs.

Time hastily paused
The flights of jolly angels,
The gates are closed
For all prosaic strangers.

Winds swirl between
The graceful birches,
Showing a postcard scene
With our steepled churches.

Bright as a burning match,
Crisp as a godsent sound,
Beyond my humble batch
A rainbow taps the ground.

The sun loudly wheeled
Into my silent room;
The envelope is sealed,
The spring must bloom.

I Want to Be Myself

I wish to play a Stradivarius violin.
I like the filigrees of prodigy Cellini.
I dream of being Huckleberry Finn.
I crave to be insane like Paganini.
I envy elongated figures of El Greco.
I cannot be Shakespeare; it's hard,
I'd rather be Beethoven's echo
Within the Russian Avant-garde;
I want to sculpt as if I am Rodin;
I long for my Tahiti like Gauguin;
I wish to paint like great Vermeer
Or be a little crazy like Van Gogh.

No, No and No! My path is clear,
I'd rather be myself before I go...

My Gloomy Fate

My doubts stroll along my quest
To stop my fall into a cozy nest.
Let's hit the road, walk me through,
Show the light, expose the fraud,
Unmask the sight, give me a clue.

Even my self-complacent vanity
Drowned in silence of the night,
Is it a premonition of calamity?
Is it a ticket for my final flight?

The top attempts to lead,
The bottom hardly follows;
A healthy future's seed
Won't grow in the shallows.

Deserted by my friends,
I am not falling on my sword:
I plow the unknown lands,
And trying to dig up the word,
Despite all odds and trends.

The trees of poetry still grow
On boneyards of contention;
The apples will forever glow,
Anticipating Eve's intention.

My rather unassuming art
Packed in a shopping cart,
The critics-cashiers wait
To check my gloomy fate.

Nostalgia Will Die or Flee

I doze during lethargic days,
I play across exciting nights.
Wisdom reveals to me,
"Get out of this maze,
Nostalgia will die or flee
Into the blinding lights."

The wedge of flying cranes
Cuts boldly through the sky,
To reach their ancient saints,
No one yet asked them why.

The loud wheels drum out
The melodies of shiny rails,
The endless boxing bout
Of time against the trains:
The trees are flying back,
My valor quickly disappears,
I am a total human wreck,
I cannot change the gears.

I gave away my kingdom,
No memories, no sorrows;
Life passes by the window
In expectation of tomorrows.

Where am I coming from?
I only spent, I didn't save,
I rambled as a careless boy,
I never even owned a home;
These days, I own a grave,
Creation of my angel's ploy.

She Knew

In our virgin bed, we sang
The songs without words,
Love was a boomerang
Between two wrongs,
Between two worlds
From the beginning
Without meaning.

She was a stream of hope
Across a quiet fertile field,
She was my horoscope,
She was my loving nurse,
She knew
My fate was sealed,
She knew
The route of my orbit,
She didn't read my verse,
She only hoarded.

I didn't like the fruits of fame,
She wouldn't post my poems
On the wall,
What's in the name?
No one deserves the blame,
All wilted roses smell the same.

My mother's precious womb
From which I sprang
Forgot the pains of birth.
I lived without ever being young,
But then, I left the planet Earth,
To live in the invented paradise
The one to which the sinners rise.

The Yoke of Wisdom

The dullness of old pains
Hovers above my grave,
The heavens cry with rains
For lives they couldn't save.

The yoke of wisdom
Collects life's choices
Under its sacred dome
Of our internal voices.

Today, I finally can do
Whatever I desire:
I bathe in morning dew
Or set the world on fire;
I even altered a few words
To suit the flow of my chords,
But when the nights are long,
I sing the same old dreary song.

I didn't try to lead the blind,
I tried to learn their dreams;
I walked my nervous mind
Among their sordid whims,
And lulled their quiet lives
With a few convoluted lies.

Even the eagles never fly
Only until the sunsets die.
Our fairs and lives will pass,
Our tomorrows will not cry:
The emeralds of fertile grass
Become the diamonds of dew
And bring us something new,
A fresher, better lie.

The Leitmotifs

My goal is frozen,
It is a soaring vanity
Of useless meetings;
My path is chosen,
It is the night's insanity
Of gambling whippings.

I saw a slot and put a quarter
Then held the reins in hand,
Pegasus flew above the land,
Into the gambling slaughter.

Casino is a miserable bride,
The Queen of broken hearts;
I grit my teeth and ride
Against the decks of cards,
And only my illusions
Will never rest in peace
In quagmires of confusions
Imagining a morning breeze.

Saint Paul was wrong;
Those who don't work
Will always get their feed,
And won't erase their smirk.
The leitmotifs of every song:
Envy, pride, vanity, and greed.

The Hazy Slopes

The hazy slopes,
The murky sights,
The wasted hopes,
In our fruitless fights.

The compass of my soul
Led me into a muddy ditch;
A chance to reach my goal.
Was wasted in that ugly pitch.

I bought my tickets every day
To watch a film named "Love";
I was an actor in that play,
To learn what we are made of.

I didn't want to hear
Your last goodbye,
I grabbed my souvenir,
It was your farewell sigh.

I didn't tell you everything,
And yet, I never lied;
Whatever you may think,
I loved; at least, I tried.

The Guilty Pleasures

Our mawkish treasures
Have been stolen,
In vain we try to find it.
The guilty pleasures
Of the brave and fallen,
Stroll close behind it.

To us, the real wisdom
Comes never or too late,
Shaped as an airy dome;
Maybe it is our lucky fate.

We can no longer bear
The yoke of our guilt,
For our concealed affair
Under a collective quilt.

Our daily pointless strive,
Turns life into a whore,
We entertain and thrive
And infinitely paid more.

Life hardly goes on,
I feverishly navigate
My way into the gate,
My efforts unopposed,
Late night, I am alone,
The sign says "closed".

The Fruit of Passion

There are no bars
Without meals,
There are no cars
Without wheels,
There is no smoke
Without a fire,
There is no cloak
To cover my desire,
And my possession
Of the cross I wear.
The fruit of passion,
The fruit of our affair
Was my aggression
And your depression
I could no longer bear.
Just plain and square.

There are no tailors
Without needles,
There are no failures
Without riddles.

There is a reason
In our love of arts,
There is a season
For broken hearts.

The cupids' darts
Pierce our hearts.

The Fogs of London Said Goodbye

The sun of Nice paraded its July,
The fogs of London said goodbye.
I hear the music of a running train,
The world is in my window's frame,
It is like a film without movie stars,
It is a war without wounds and scars.

My problems choke me like a noose,
My glass is full, my heart is empty,
The waiter bending like a goose,
He thinks I own the Horn of Plenty.

I knew the heroes and the villains,
I knew my punishments and crimes,
I am grateful to those who gave us
The trains tapping their jolly rhymes.

The train tries to erase our daily stress,
All petty problems swirl into the drain,
All passengers look happy and I guess,
Their guarding angels follow our train.

Plus, minus, good, evil, dark and light,
This well established order never fails,
The trains of lives take us into the night,
We love the rhythmic rhapsodies of rails.

The rails are raked and lined
Straight like the summer rains,
We left our losses far behind,
We see mirages of the gains.

We never meet a stranger on the train,
We talk and laugh, we share our stories,
We say goodbye and never meet again,
We're candid and sincere without worries;
The train is a conspirator in our magic ploy,
It turns a year of boredom into a day of joy.

The Frozen Sun

No clouds in the sky,
Only the sun and I.

I am shuddering alone
Under the frozen sun
Next to an old tombstone,
Abandoned by someone.

I wanted every night
Forever to be first,
I didn't want daylight
To satisfy my thirst.

I heard the nightingales
Above the sunset trails,
I heard the crying violins
Concealing nightly sins.

These puzzling gestures
Of a mime
Don't reach my idle ears,
Although an ancient voice
Of time
Foretold my devastating
Years.
When innocence commits
A crime,
Only the sinners shed their
Tears.

Beyond the window frost,
I will ascend into a place
Where our eternal host
Will wrap me in his grace.

Higher Than the Skies

I veered around common sense,
Virtue and vice of my hometown;
I didn't have or missed a chance
To climb the tree of knowledge
And to admire the tree of life;
Somebody took them down,
The others locked the gate
And said, "Heaven can wait."

The maps of journeys to nowhere
Are sealed in a godsent envelope;
There is infinity of my despair,
There is my never-ending hope
To always know when and where.

Nevertheless, my train arrived
Into the promised Horn of Plenty;
I hopelessly and sadly smiled,
My mind and heart were empty.

My soul flies higher than the skies,
Nobody mourns, nobody cries;
My body rots below the grass,
God shines my tombstone's brass.

The sun lights edges of the cloud
Above the heads of crowned kings;
I left on Earth my tattered shroud,
And grow a pair of mighty wings...

The Fat Lady Sings.

Skyscrapers cast long shadows,
The darkness blanks our minds,
Statistics show ups and downs,
We work until our time rewinds.

A naked body lying on the street,
I robbed and killed that stranger;
Unnerving image of an urban beat,
Looks like a wingless fallen angel.

I am a captive of my own despair:
I am sick and tired of my crimes,
I am someone who loves fresh air,
But I never valued human lives.

The kingdom of nightmares,
The tribal rules and attitudes:
One turns a cheek and prays,
Some kill to solve their feuds.

I stroll along death row,
The saddest of the trails,
I wait and watch the flow
Of the final nights and days.

This dreary supper is my last,
I did the crime, I did the time,
There is no future, just a past,
Am I still worthy of a dime?

I crave a sympathetic sigh,
The grimace of a sorrow,
A whisper or a silent cry,
As echo of a sad tomorrow.

An executer turns the switch,
They hide from me that sight,
I only see a fat and ugly witch,
The lady sings, I take the flight.

Skyscraper cast long shadows,
The darkness blocks my mind,
Statistics show ups and downs,
Meanwhile, I left my life behind.

The Heavens are Still Bare

Two birds, two tired souls,
Two dreams, two hopes,
Two schemes, two goals,
Two fighters on the ropes.

Two friends, a single ride,
Eternal carousel of pride.

I am throwing a no-hitter,
Dogs fighting for a bone;
You are still grossly bitter,
And aim at me your stone.

I canceled yesterdays,
I don't expect tomorrows,
I breathe my glee today
Avoiding ills and sorrows.

I hover as a flying saucer,
I can't elect to stop or go,
I couldn't fly much closer,
I feared your blinding glow.

You couldn't ever suffer,
You wouldn't hate or love
Unless a life gets tougher
And drops its velvet glove.

The jury is already out,
A foreman is not mute:
"Your marriage died
In a devastating drought,
It needs an olden shroud
Or just a graveyard suit".

You never needed anyone,
You never had a real flare;
Though since you are gone,
The heavens are still bare.

A House of Cards

A house of cards,
A fragile paradise for men,
Who never trust the guards
And preachers muttering amen.

There are no lintels,
No roofs, no walls,
No snowy winters
No golden falls;
Just sunny springs
And sultry summers,
A pair of wedding rings
And marriage-slammers.

The sizzling truths and lies
Lead to a bar or to a church,
My Leo sign above our strives
Points to a bar, not to a church.

The churches' steeples
Poked the virgin skies,
My girlfriend's nipples
Reflected in my eyes.

I made my choice,
I have no other wish,
I hear my inner voice,
"Stop drinking like a fish!"

There Is a Corner in My Heart

There is a corner in my heart,
A little room for a dear friend:
The rest of me was set apart
From everyone I've ever met.

I went to see my friend,
The cemetery was dark,
The silence held my hand,
The branches shaped an arc.

We walked our own poetic roads,
I never understood his verses:
He carved his sentimental odes,
I scratched my senseless curses;
I laughed when he would cry,
I crawled, but he could fly.

I'd walk away, but he would stay,
I fought, but he would pray.
We used to call each other brother,
And if I cursed; he'd say "Our Father..."

It has been said, time dulls our pain,
Life moves ahead, departs in vain,
Time passed, I went to see my friend,
A mourning silence held my hand.

The Wrath of Your Farewell

I used to turn those sparkly stars
Into the flowers for your bouquet,
You were an actress of the farce,
Then fled into the winds of May.

The wrath of your farewell
Appeased my wounds;
While you were raising hell,
I heard the pacifying tunes.
.
Today, an old nostalgic metronome
Evokes the rhythm of my heartbeat;
I imitate the Romans while in Rome:
I date and dance, I drink and eat...

The Clouds Part

Reality is gravely ill,
Reality is too obscure,
I am surreal if you will,
I had revealed a cure:
The clouds part,
The beam of sun
Pierces my heart
And fear is gone.

The heart of my nightmare,
The graveyard of my soul,
The bridge into nowhere
Entombed in a quagmire
But really wanted to unroll
The flames from a bonfire.

Please, cease a candlelight,
A day may morph into a night,
And I will exercise my whim
To coach a fireball to swim
Lengthwise the curly stream
Into the river of my dream.

I am old, my hair is gray,
No skin in a lifetime play;
In front of an empty dish,
Stars fall; I have no wish.

The Early Snow Strolls

The early snow strolls
Over my forgiven sins,
Pure as the naked souls
Of virgins in the whites,
Pure as glory of my wins
I can no longer trace,
As darkness of my nights,
As lightness of my days.

I visit many old addresses,
I walk across old bridges,
I crave old joys and stresses,
I long for luminous old ridges.

I laugh a lot, I can no longer cry,
I've seen it all, my eyes are dry,
I've known love that never ends,
I wish it to my foes and friends.

I am poet with a naked soul,
I breathe; you think I sigh,
They wanted me to crawl;
As Icarus I learned to fly.

I lived through cunning treasons,
I loved deviations of all seasons,
I dreamed, I fought and I survived,
I reached the threshold of my life.
Hello, goodbye; I've finally arrived.

No one yet heard the word,
I ceased my lifelong chase,
At night, I'll reach His world,
At dawn, I'll touch His face.

New Christmas Fever

New Christmas fever
Consumes our lives,
The moonlight's silver
Reflecting in her eyes.

Two candles burn
Their nights on tables,
Meanwhile I try to earn
Appreciation in her fables.

Religion serves its gelded
Willfully blind compliance,
Psychologists are welded
To traps of pseudoscience.

I caught the final breath
Of my daily prayer;
Which was already frail
And picked a mask of death,
Which was too old to wear,
As old as the Holy Grail
Held by lovely mistress.
She whispered in my ear,
"I wish you
A Merry Christmas,
I wish you
A Joyful New Year!"

I didn't try to flee,
I played a hide and seek
With my untarnished glee;
The Bible firmly asked,
I turned the other cheek;
I am no longer masked
I am no longer weak.

I Hear a Sober Voice

I hear a sober voice:
There are no cowboys,
There are no cows,
Just a few bolding boys
Playing cat and mouse.

And yet it is much worse.
They cannot ride a horse;
They drive electric cars,
And drink a nonfat yogurt
In the bars.

Some feathers to be roughed,
Some rascals will be cuffed,
The equilibrium preserved,
Our society is nicely served.

Spaghetti Westerns
Instead of daily strives,
Blood of ancestors
Drained from our lives.

The ship of fools
Drifts in the sea;
No skills, no tools,
Long live our glee!

Start Drinking

Complexity of structure,
Dark berries' rupture,
The supple aromatics
Appear quite busy;
Linguistic acrobatics
Make even me too dizzy.

A breeze of apples is too crude,
The ripen cherries briefly pose
Some hints of caramel and fruit,
A trace of daises on the nose.

Vanilla of the French oaks,
Wild flowers, banana peels,
Inferiority of Spanish corks,
Nice labels, regional appeals.

The lime strikes as a mallet,
Sugary legs, lingering spices
Barely affect somebody's pallet,
But naturally elevate the prices.

The terroir and midday winds,
Acidity of tannins on the gums,
The ends of a few famous bins,
Dark chocolate and winter mums.

Hey, connoisseurs of wine,
Stop talking like doorknobs,
You are not friends of mine,
Start drinking, stupid snobs.

The Darkness is So Bright

We rest through Sundays,
Mondays are just as bad,
Then land on our runways
In search for daily bread.

The darkness of the night
Nursing a baby-dawn
Before the farewell flight,
We kiss and we are gone.

Our euphoric angels hide;
Delusions fade so fast;
Blind leads the blind;
Our marriages don't last.
After we accidentally find
The cliff of our great divide.

Our fates' iron wills
Morphed our night
Into a sunny day.
I simply paid the bills
For our farewell flight
To join the birds of prey.

I placed my lucky bet
Against the red sunset,
I am happy, I can write,
The darkness is so bright.

The Dangling Diamonds

The dangling diamonds
Tease our dog-tired eyes;
It is a fragile naughty joy,
The treacherous thin ice
Of downtown tango dives,
And elegance of dresses,
Wrapping the hollow lives
Of daily made princesses.

It is a tiny slice of living,
Of chosen for the loop,
It is a nightly final inning
For a newsworthy scoop.

I'd take our modish clubs
With French champagne
Versus the beery Irish pubs
And let them flaunt the pain.

I Push Reality Aside

I paraphrase Simone de Beauvoir:
"You always know who you are,
If you desire, change life today,
Don't gamble on tomorrows;
There's no future, don't delay,
No one will soothe your sorrows."

I take a tiny bit
Of what I have been given;
Then morphed it
Into a person driven
To learn the word
And start another world.

I make my art until I faint.
I'd rather write than paint.
But in a book or in a frame,
Both efforts look the same.

No one reserved a space
For art in a protected haven,
We often pick a babyface,
Ignoring an unattractive raven.

I meander in the middle,
I try to solve the riddle
Of the eternal universe;
I paint or carve a verse.

I push reality aside.
I try to cut the cord,
Then soar or slide
Into a better world
So artfully created.

Where is it located?

I Only Hear the Thunder

When I've been sick,
I never called a doctor,
I never called a friend,
I knew an ancient trick
For every skinless actor
On life-is-a-theatre stage:
Before your life is ripped,
Don't seek a caring hand,
Please, read the script,
There is a second page.

I felt a shooting pain
In my left arm,
I broke my rule and called;
My doc infused his brain,
And mumbled in the cold,
"I pledged to do no harm."

Deaths all around me
As far as one can see.
And yet I've got a real gift,
I will become a saint today,
I will be virtuous and swift.
Just wait, I am on the way
To be a hero who can fold,
My bliss no more; Too old.

I think, I am six feet under;
I cannot see the lightning,
I only hear the thunder,
At last, I am not fighting.
I left my heart and soul
Descending from the hill,
I reached my parting goal,
Tonight, I'll sign my will.

Spring's ready to arrive,
A red cardinal will fight
His own reflection;
The flowers will thrive,
The sun is kindly bright
And rolls in my direction.
Is it the face of joy and love:
An iron fist in a velvet glove?

I Moved into LA

A perfect place
Under the sun,
A striking face,
A sweetie bun,
Lives in the valley,
Her name is Holly.

I want to live in Hollywood,
I asked, but Holly wouldn't.
She wonders if she should,
I wonder if she shouldn't.
Our destiny is not our fate,
I see no issues at the gate.

It was one of my restless nights,
I fixed a car and moved into LA
To watch those blinding lights
Cascading just above the fray,
Over these bloody futile fights
Where vivid colors kill the gray.

I am a nauseous dreamer,
I am a clever Southern boy,
Their grass seems greener,
I surely gamble with my ploy,
I split the hairs much thinner,
I enter on the horse of Troy,
I want to be a famous winner,
Holly will love this country boy.

I Overshot the Runway

Under a total moon eclipse,
From early dusk to dawn,
Four Horses of Apocalypse
Just trotted and were gone.

They plunged into the abyss
Of waterless forsaken well,
Taking the gold of maple trees
To dungeons where they dwell.

Don't wait for the next eclipse,
You'll miss the wedding bells;
Don't hide your honey lips
Like pearls inside the shells.

I knelt; looked in your eyes
And bravely threw the dice:
You're my altruistic spring
Wrapped in a silky blanket;
Here is your diamond ring
And invitations to a banquet.

Another knot is tied,
Another starry night,
Another tight embrace,
Another golden cage,
The key is laid aside;
As old as the hills,
Another apple's bite,
I kissed her baby-face:
Old book-- new page,
The same old thrills.

I overshot the runway,
My love will die in vain,
Only the trees still sway,
The world remains insane.

I Paid My Final Bill

Rain whips my windshield,
My truck rolls in the storm
Across the muddy field
Through dusk; I am alone.

Time dressed a sunny day
In a tuxedo of the night;
The radio enjoys "My way",
A sentimental ageless bite.

I am munching on my past,
It tastes sour-bitter-sweet,
I am hungry and eating fast,
I am slow only on my feet.

I am a captain on the bridge,
The ocean of my life is vast,
I am at my journey's fringe,
And meander to my final rest.

Venus rocked on the shell,
Winged Icarus already fell,
King Midas touched my boat,
He knew, gold will never float.

Nevertheless,
It was a lovely day,
I signed my living will;
In my distress
I chose "My Way",
And paid my final bill.

We Never Have to Bark

My strange nightmare:
I walk across the blaze,
My fortune sheers
Under your fiery glare.
I cloak my face
With salty tears.

I am a guardian angel
Above the rising billows;
I am a sympathetic ranger
Above the weeping willows.

I fall and crawl,
I stand and fall,
I climb and fly,
I walk…
I hover in the sky,
I am a red-tailed hawk…

A red sunset sent its adieu,
Decisions come at nights;
I am here ahead of you,
We have to end our fights.

Some wander in the dark,
Some kiss the ugly frogs,
Why do we have to bark?
For that we have our dogs.

We are not vandals,
We have to make amends,
We cannot burn our candles
From both ends.

I Only Read the Glossy Pages

Few impish children miss the cavalcade,
The elephants and horses disappeared,
The circus left, only the clowns stayed
To entertain the aged. Isn't it weird?

Great ignorance and vague confusion
Deliver confidence and arrogance to me,
I wouldn't abdicate my grand illusions,
I wouldn't have those clowns for my glee.

New days imprisoned me with pessimism
Around callous truths and bad decisions,
Establishing defeatist policies of nihilism,
Rejecting ancient principles and visions.

I left my judgements in the weeds,
Maintaining a few rosy expectations,
Believing that my enemy concedes
A truce amid a fortitude and patience.

There're some truths
That cannot be denied,
There're too many lies
That cannot be avoided.
By us or our countless foes,
Even by the feisty those
Who've been appointed
To prove me wrong. They tried…

My wicked mind relearned to laugh
At its convoluted past on my behalf;
I haven't been true to myself in ages,
I've read only the daily glossy pages.

I lived this life before,
I chose my parents well;
No one is living anymore,
I wonder where they dwell.

I Own the Morning After

Same parties, same black ties,
Same couples, same distress,
Same boring girls and guys,
Same make-believe clichés.

Small talk is a hollow drum
With only an emptiness inside,
The stupid vis-à-vis the dumb
I've had enough, I really tried.

I am a green-eyed faun,
My dreams are brusque,
I mourn and cry at dawn,
I smile and laugh at dusk.

I own the morning after,
I own my days and nights,
I own my cry and laughter,
I own my wrongs and rights.

Life is a charming song
Of turning shiny wheels
Above the dusty bridges,
Of an unknown tongue,
Of blue mysterious hills
Lined up as hazy ridges.

A plentiful cheerful fest,
Triumphant luscious wine,
A journey with my friends,
We climb the snowy Everest,
We see the sign of all divine.

As Pilate, I'll wash my hands.

I Outlived my Guilt

I chose a long way home,
My lucky star abruptly fell
But tartly asked:
"Where are you from?"
I faintly masked:
"I am ok, but lived in hell,
I barely managed there,
I wasn't blinded by the flare."

I'll be brief:
"I wrote love letters
To my babysitter,
But never mailed;
I feel as if
This really matters,
I tried to pitch a no-hitter
All my life, but failed."

I outlived my guilt,
My plastic flowers
Would never wilt,
I seldom take my showers,
I know what to drink or eat,
I know when to use my wit,
I know what I like and hate.
A joy? I can no longer wait.

The dogs of wasted years
Gathered to bark and bite,
I need to change the gears.
Get ready for my final flight.

I Shook Their Tree

Submissive cunning servants,
The human brainless pigeons,
The horde of greedy perverts
Usurping organized religions.

I have no cross to bear,
I have no cloak to wear.

I live among this Sunday flock
Whose sins are wrapped in silk;
Self-righteous pompous fools,
They stop our perpetual clock,
They curdle our Mothers' milk,
They're the Armageddon's tools.

They judge, they kick, they burn,
You have a cheek-- don't turn.

Nobody yet confessed;
Compassion is rehearsed,
Pseudo intensity injected
Into fanatically obsessed,
The outcome reversed,
Their honesty rejected.

Their insincerity of passion
Pursuing their satanic role,
Nourishes their raw aggression
And churns it out of control.

I shook their tree to pick the fruit;
At last, I'm free to dump that loot.

Elegy

Les bouquinistes vendent Hugo, Balzac, Flaubert,
I love them all, it's our forever lasting love affair,
Under the bridge, the river Seine runs its muddy water
And welcomes us to pace or comb the Latin Quarter.

A rainy day in Paris, its streets are wet,
I'm revisiting my memories of glee,
The majesty of puzzling Conciergerie,
Marquis de Sade, Marie Antoinette.

The grandeur of D'Orsey still gleams,
Together we relish our happy dreams;
Old riverboats burn with the sun,
It is our final day. The end is near, we run.

Pont Neuf my arm is on your shoulder,
My fingers walk across your silky hair.
I cannot sense that our days were over,
I can't imagine that; I wouldn't even dare.

Those days are gone and took my honeyed treats,
I carried on, so many sleepless nights passed by,
So many winds swept through the dusty streets,
It's so impossible to love and to be wise, but why?

The end: I'm the one to blame.
An intuition of a hollow wisdom
Has left the station as the train.
My sacrament is still the same.
I keep or leave this kingdom;
I live a life or disappear in vain.

I Miss the Heat

I rubbed the sparkly lamp,
I only dug Aladdin's gold
Behind the highway ramp,
I didn't pick it up--too cold.

Forget the spring,
The winter rolls,
The snow falls
On our street.

I miss the heat;
And throw my hat
Into the ring:
I sip Jack Daniels and sing
A song of winter's threat,
And think about sunny rays,
And play my whiny old guitar,
And hop the calendar of days
Towards the spring; it isn't far.

I only dug Aladdin's gold;
I didn't pick it up--too cold.

I Miss You, Dear

I miss you, dear,
Wait; I'll come home
At dinnertime;
Our planet's sphere
Allows me to roam
And u-turn on a dime.

The drumming wheels
Of hurrying trains
Wake tempting visions
Of vast, abundant planes,
Of sun-drenched seasons,
Of castles in the clouds,
Of thoughts and doubts.

My train is moving straight,
Although, the railroad veers,
I hope, it's not too late
To ride a few more years.

Its looming silhouette
Moves life into reset,
I can no longer bear
A life on chemin de fer.

I miss you, dear,
Just wait,
I am coming home;
I'll cross the sphere,
And you will say shalom.

I Ride the Rollercoasters

The sun parades its grin,
I am devouring its flow,
I am basking in its sheen,
I am blinded by its glow.

Some crispy bacon
Along the sunny side,
I cannot even recon
A better-looking sight.

I never rest on laurels,
I ride the rollercoasters,
I leave my quarrels
To babies on the posters.

I am a sword of steel,
I am a fiery navy seal;
I have a needed skill,
If you won't fight, I will.

Some lose my trust,
Some follow an advice,
Some satisfy my lust,
Some only tease my eyes.

Some build their wealth,
They lay a base, expend,
Refine and reconstruct;
They lose their health,
Collect, don't ever spend,
They're hollow as a duct.

I wear a military gear,
I'll avoid the slaughters,
I'll sail with you from fear
Across the Sea of Galilee;
I'll dare to walk on waters
And lead you to a glee.

I Run My Circles

I run my circles and zigzags,
Around these lethargic fakers;
They wear the orange tags
Of hopeless troublemakers.

No one will ever help,
Don't ever scream,
Don't bump your head,
Don't ever whisper.
A piece of bread
No one will spare,
The dogs will yelp,
The moon will gleam.

Don't try to flee,
Just dance with me,
It is our first journey;
It's only you and me,
Just hug and kiss me,
Make it a night of glee.

.

It was a nasty theft;
He stole your heart,
You were his prey,
He killed and left.
Love is a dying art
On feet of clay.

I Sailed to a Dazzling Capri

I sailed to a dazzling Capri,
The isle of lemon vapors,
I went to Positano and Amalfi,
But fell in love with dusty Naples.

I am back to cheerful Sorrento,
Draped in the shawl of night;
I grabbed a bite and went to
Walk the corridors of light.

I hear the famous music boxes
Inlaid with lacy filigree of wood,
This polished glittery of phloxes
Lives in the garden of my mood.

I love the Sud, the South
With sunlit rocky bluffs,
Next to Vesuvius' big mouth
That blows to the sky its puffs.

I veer amid Pompei's old bordellos,
These ruined dungeons of delights,
Among the hordes of other fellows,
Preferring so-called wrongs to rights.

And finally, the end of summer,
My poor Italian is rather silly;
Please, disregard my grammar,
"Amore, ciao, grazie mile."

I Reaped a Hurricane

I sowed a wind,
I reaped a hurricane;
I lived and truly sinned,
It was the devil's gain.

I drift between the souls,
I'm a boat without the sails,
I lost my aims and goals,
I'm a train without the rails.

In the periphery of life,
I am still a second best;
I would prefer to strife
Or vanish as all the rest.

The valor of a foolish child
Alone against the tides,
I am determent, I am wild;
I am in the pursuit of fights.

My life is fauna wrapped
In flora,
I crave a tiny bit of ecstasy
In every day,
When I am ready for a jovial
Tomorrow,
I'll climb the bright celestial
Stairway.

I Learned the Real Price

The moment will arise
When we are asked
To pay a hefty price
For what we only guess
Its real worth:
At first as birth
Of love and happiness,
At last as death;
We sowed our kindness,
Why did we reap
Our love's final breath?

Your love is gone,
I read your face;
You have someone
To take my place.

I walked into the door,
I learned the real price
Of a depressing war,
But not of paradise.

I Prayed for Only One

I heard, my grandma said,
"The skies are for the stars,
Wine likes a lavish spread,
While vodkas like the bars."

I celebrate
My heartfelt hospitality,
I celebrate
My energetic curiosity,
I mourn the end
Of my unending life,
My godsend immortality
Still wanders next to me
Dead or alive.

I am a leafless tree,
I stand alone at night,
Please, come to me,
Bring me some light.

No one can kiss their own
Forehead,
No one can enter rolling
Rivers twice,
I am alone in my cold bed,
Though, I am forever free,
I tossed my lucky dice,
Two rows, three and three.

The angels fall,
The birds still fly,
The birds still sing
Amazing grace
To every soul

Of those who've gone,
The bells still ring,
But why?
Because
I prayed for only one."

I Pay in Life for Every Pleasure

I am tired of the books I've read,
I craved to breathe a fresher air,
I learned to earn my daily bread,
I am the fallen angel's heir...

The lights are flashing,
The sirens briskly blaring,
The sight is smashing,
My guiltiness is glaring.
I pulled onto a dusty shoulder,
And pulled my driver's license;
A cop wrote a citation in his folder
Gave it to me and smiled in silence.

Along the highway of my life,
Over the valleys and the hills;
I heal my wounds after a strife,
Life is a college for my skills.

A maven said,
"Don't blame a mirror
When you are ugly."
Too bad,
I am not a real hero:
I pay and drown in my bubbly.

Life never gives away free lunches,
Life blows kisses or hard punches.
I pay in life for every pleasure,
But freedom is my only treasure.

Saint Catherine

A bride of God, Saint Cat,
You kept your word
Against the deadly threat
From our corrupted world.

You kept your sacred ring,
You took it to the wheel,
Your marriage to the King
Survived your final meal.

You lost your head,
God saved your soul;
Young fearless Cat,
You outlived us all.

The proud Alexandrian,
You kept your ring,
You are a loyal guardian
Of our vows to the King.

Plea

We live, we learn,
We drop some tears,
We fight, we suffer,
The wreckage looms;
The memories return,
And bring those years:
My scars got rougher
Than my bloody wounds.

Smoke leaves the flute,
It warms my cooler days;
You were so artfully cute,
But didn't leave a trace.

The wars remain behind,
The bullet whistles gone;
Our sentences were signed
Between the dusk and dawn.

Love lost another strife,
Love lost its final breath,
Life is a flight above the sea,
Death is an answer to a plea.

Spring Thaw

Life craves to dust and bathe
Our predetermined faith,
But teaches us to laugh or cry
We learn to die then fly.

Three giants of existence,
Our opinions and our doubts
Run their eternal distance
From births to final shrouds.

Just ask the dead,
Life's awfully short,
Today, you are a newlywed,
Tomorrow, a divorcee in court.

Don't pray for rain,
Just wash your car.
Don't heal the pain,
Drink in a local bar.
Don't whine in vain,
Rapture's pretty far,
Eat your free lunch,
Just ask how much.

A custom of spring thaw:
The ice and snow melt,
The creeks already flow,
Old winter locks its belt,
Frost runs a narrow path
And veils its bitter wrath.

Rejoice the rite of spring,
Don't be too sad, c'mon,
The Easter bells will ring,
You'll see another dawn.

Shenandoah

The quiet river Shenandoah,
A daughter of the shiny stars,
I love the grandeur of your flow,
The song of a thousand guitars.

I love the striking valley on the river,
There must be a divine caregiver;
The fall of blossoms from your trees
Reminds of snowflakes in dizzy spins,
The kindly merciless morning freeze
Grants gentle petals to the winds,
Looking like tickets of wasted bets,
Crumpled and thrown on the floor;
This fluffy snow gradually melts
As if a weary winter lost its war.

Virginia and Shenandoah,
Two proudly sunny stars,
It is only a stone's throw
To our history and scars.

I Beg You, Do Not Breed

The winter wanders
In my exhausted soul,
The hungry condors
Still waiting for my fall.

Poor nouveau riche,
They eat until it hurts:
A comedy in every dish,
A boredom for desserts.

They try to justify their greed
To their dumb feeders,
Whether they stand or crawl.
Regrettably, through history,
Sleaze-balls succeed;
It's not a mystery,
The bottom feeders
Have no room to fall.

Their guidance from A to Z
Created a society of greed;
Hurrah to you, Bourgeoisie.

I beg you, "Do not breed."

I Walked Before I Crawled

I walked before I crawled,
I climbed the rainbow arc,
I saw my future sprawled.
Why do I ramble in the dark?

There's nothing more permanent
Than temporary changes.
Life is a never-ending tournament
Flanked by the shooting ranges.

I faced the wrath of living gods,
Survived and left it far behind.
I veered amid the lightning rods,
Relying on my tempered mind.

There's someone I am dating,
A one who wants to be my wife,
The one for whom I am waiting
All my life.

A honey to my eyes and ears,
We talked and drank a few
To catch some wasted years.
A party started with a bang:
After a dance, I grabbed a mike,
Inhaled and sang
The only song I knew...
The only song she didn't like.

I drowned
In a bottomless whirlpool
Of her unforgiving eyes.
Tonight, I am crowned
As a village idiot and fool,
A one trick pony in disguise.

I am a mindless bodyguard
Of a capricious wind-up doll.
I am not a poet, not a bard,
I am not a thunder, not a fireball.
But I am a gambler. No regrets.
The others placed their bets.

.

I Want to Be a Clown

We're on horsebacks
Cross our rivers-lives,
Nobody changed their
Horses in the middle,
It's not a trendy show,
But our daily strides
We fight; nobody plays
A fiddle.

The loud streetlights
Glow with madness;
We stroll at nights
Embracing sadness;
Life vigorously bites
Our blissful badness.

We have surrendered
To our foes
In spite of being armed
And feared,
Daily confessions and
Remorse
Won't change our tired
Laws.
They're already cooked
And sealed.
No one can ride or stop
What no one knows.

Teardrops run down
And slake the wicks,
A loud coo-coo clock
Drums out tic-tac-tics
Over the foolish flock.

I want to be a clown.

I am a Polyglot

I am a polyglot,
I am a devil in disguise,
I have a secret plot,
A French girl is a prize.

I speak and understand
Some foreign tongues;
My French girlfriend
Wears orange thongs...

I've got a great advice, a pearl:
"Don't ever miss your turn,
Make love to your interpreter
If you desire a tongue to learn."

Too many girls,
Too little time,
I hired a head nurse
To get ahead in line.

I speak and understand
Some foreign tongues,
My Indonesian girlfriend
Wears purple thongs...

I Sinned

The Queens of hearts
And spades,
The Kings on Thrones,
None of them earned
High grades,
I sinned, they cast
The stones.

They left their wreck
To slap my poker face,
I used a loaded deck,
But never left a trace.

I went over my grief,
My blood still churns,
I am treated as a thief,
The bridge still burns.

I have my breaking point,
That line I mustn't cross,
I smoke my sacred joint,scd
It says, "I am still the boss."

That bargain had two ends
Even in a gambling world,
I held mine with two hands,
I learned to keep my word.

Am I a loser or a winner?
Am I a gambler-sinner?
A junior ice-cold croupier
Still counts uno, due, tre…

s

I Spilled a Glass of Wine

I pushed a man of the cloth,
And spilled a glass of wine
Over his tired wrinkled soul,
He noticed, but didn't blink.
We waited in the line,
We had the best of all,
We had a lovely drink,
Espresso with a froth.

I look much younger
Than my peers,
Life has a compelling reason
God never counted the years
I spent in prison.

My history unfolds,
Yet effortlessly holds
Its metaphysical allure;
We all will fall, I'm sure,
Into the morbid molds
Before a psychiatric cure.

We all are shameless actors,
I am a director of that theatre;
I watch a bouncing dead cat,
And thinking through my hat
That I am exuberantly proud
Of gifted, well acting Heroes,
But in a demi season drought,
I put on stage the futile Zeros.
Life goes on. Life is a theatre.

Another spring in hand,
Old winter left the cage,
Life is a marching band
Of cretins on the stage.

Only the Shadows Never Die

Intriguing anguish of your glance
Invites the thirst of my frail soul,
The night is young, let's dance
And let our shadows stroll.

Embrace me in a single dance,
We'll unfurl our wings and fly,
Unite us in a second chance,
Let our passion reach the sky.

The apple of contention
Fell from the tree of love:
Another good intention,
Another loveless dove,
Another great dissention,
Another shameful farewell
Paved our alleyway to hell.

It was our last romance,
It was our great endeavor,
It is our farewell dance,
Only the shadows live forever.

We're immortal only for a while,
Then slowly vanish one by one,
Only two quiet arrows on a dial
Maintain a single lifelong run.

It is our mortal run, get high,
Only the shadows never die.

Those Valued Lessons

I marched into my adolescence,
I've met a few attractive women
Who gave me many jolly lessons
About love, orgasms and semen.

As a new father of the nation,
I couldn't feed that many kids;
After a pointed conversation
I sent to Santa all their needs.

My kids enjoyed their adolescence,
They learned those valued lessons;
Long live this everlasting college,
The Holy Grail of carnal knowledge.

Surrounded by narrow-minded Philistines,
I gave some extra education to my teens.

Paradise Lost

Some play the hearts,
Some make the deals,
Some benefit the arts,
Some turn the wheels.

Some read the news
And shrug their shoulders;
Fake news, unreal.
The old volcano spews
Fiery truck-sized boulders;
Who cares, big deal.

I wasn't preaching to the choir,
They weren't taken by surprise:
Their lives lost an essential fire,
They lost their earthly paradise.

I am a death-row lifer,
I've read the book of fate,
I was too slow to decipher,
Those words. Is it too late?

I sailed along these years,
And tried to do my best;
I curbed my fears and tears,
But flunked the final test:
I just misplaced my pair of dice
And lost the promised paradise.

Paradise Found

Without early warning,
Dawn sent its baby-ray
Through maple leaves,
Hello, another morning.
The stars abruptly left,
But didn't say goodbye,
They are extremely deft,
They'll certainly drop by.

I scrambled a few eggs,
Sautéed some bacon;
My dog wiggles his tail
And passionately begs;
He is absolutely faking,
I understand his Braille.

A brave-heart albatross
Hovers above the ridge.
I'd rather drag a cross
Than burn that bridge.

I suffered many pains,
I won't forgive;
I had so many gains
I want to give
To those who truly tried,
But didn't have a guide.

I am like a golden leaf,
I happily swirl around,
I soar above my grief.
Paradise lost? I found.

Over the Old Thresholds

The boundaries of trust
From a forgotten dream:
My soul was lying in the dust,
My body crossed the stream.

I went to quiet paradise
Over the old thresholds,
Over the misery of lives;
Where our truth unfolds,
Where nobody tells lies.

The sins of our brothers
Stain even clouded days,
The faith of our fathers
Leads to eternity of grace.

My boots are pointy-toed,
Another path, another road,
Another half of our Earth,
Another life, another birth.

I am not a foreigner,
I am a weary broom
Which knows every corner
In every dusty room.
I am like a good old friend,
Reliable and loyal to the end.
I have a straightforward mind,
I am an artless judge. I am blind.

Out of This World

She was so slender and so tall,
The regal swan's willowy grace,
I asked her, "Didn't you ever fall
On our planet from outer space?"
She didn't mind at all
And plainly answered:" Yes."

I knew she was not kidding
With this utterly quirky fable,
But she was positively willing
And I was definitely able…

Say nothing, take my word,
Our night was out of this world.

Our Southern Drawl

The ragged thunderclouds
Brew over my sinful head,
The raindrops hit the grounds
Like teardrops made of lead.

They fought for worthless goals,
I touched their wounds and scars,
I laid to rest my fallen brothers,
And watched their tortured souls
Soared into the trembling arms
Of their heartbroken mothers.

The days were sour,
I couldn't write or sing,
Yet a cold winter passed,
Only the memories still last
Like this dried out fragile flower
Between the pages of that spring.

Here comes the sun,
Those days have gone;
The fertile valleys sprawl
Just like our Southern drawl.

She was so Young and Fresh

She was so young and fresh,
Even her knees were scratched;
A tender flower in flawless flesh
Her eyes and heavens matched.

Against her charm and beauty
There was no valuable defense:
She was nineteen, a real cutie,
We kissed and flew to France.

I ate her with the spoon,
I dived into my youth again,
I am not a nerd, I am a goon,
Nothing to lose, only to gain.

The merciless sound of alarm
Was loud as a cow on the farm;
When I woke up, I sadly wept,
It was my lovely dream. I slept.

She Wasn't There

There is no free lunch,
Even in France:
"Just tell me how much
For love after this dance."

I love Parisian hookers,
Their pimps, their bookers
That work Rue Saint-Denis,
A haven of my nightly glee.

"Don't tell me
C'est la guerre,
It's war, life is unfair,
Don't offer me
Ménage a trois.
It isn't yet my last hurrah.
Just come to bed."
"I love you, too", she said.

But when I woke,
She wasn't there,
I rolled and lit a smoke,
Annoyed as an April hare.

At noon, she has returned,
And like a preacher looked
Directly in my eyes
Then calmly said:
"I am entirely booked,
I'll see you in the skies;
For now, go back to bed;
So long, I work the Gars,
It is my ghostly world,

Your stars and bars
Are yet unfurled."

I queried, "De nouveau?
Anew?"
She smiled, "I have to go."

We Watch Firsthand

The sky loves land,
The union of equals,
We watch firsthand
A mystery of sequels.

Two stars, one hope,
Two czars, one rope.

The sky is everywhere:
West, south, east or north,
Land also dwells up there,
Sways back and forth,
Looks like a love affair
For what it's worth.

These are two flames,
They burn each other,
They play the games:
The fights don't bother
Their self-inflicted pain.

Nobody dances in the rain.

The tired winter's throw
Can't hide fast streams
Amid the melting snow,
A hurried water gleams.

During the springs
Land loves the sky;
No wedding rings,
No wedding pie.

My Youth Abandoned Me

I am back to my beloved Nice,
Rains piercing my umbrella,
Trees crying on the streets,
I came to see Henri Matisse,
Chagall's incomparable Bella,
Besides some topless treats.

My youth abandoned me,
Vanity has risen to its crest,
I am still in a pursuit of glee,
But hardly ever do my best.
My efforts burst in flames,
Dawn didn't paint the skies,
But whispered a few names
Of friendly devils in disguise.

My soul lives in tomorrows,
My body's resting in the past,
I only guess, God knows
When joy will visit me, at last.

I lived, being an optimist,
I never smoked the grass
Quite certain of ascending.
Today, I am a pessimist
And fervently demanding
My parting coup de grace.

No more pageboys
And flower girls,
Deaths prancing through
The crowds,
Some kissed goodbye
Their diamonds and pearls,

I kissed goodbye my fears
And doubts.
I won't be back, my Nice.
Goodbye, divine Chagall,
Goodbye divine Matisse.

Nashville Limerick

At night, in Nashville's downtown
I drank a lot and tried to drown,
Then met a real Southern belle,
Unfortunately, she came from hell.

She had a squeaky-hinges voice,
She was a Springfield's witch,
She's gotten loud and quite tipsy,
I offered her an honorable choice
To bitch or not to bitch…
Guess what, she whistled Dixie.

I took her to a yellow cab,
I paid; I touched her lovely legs:
Instead of silky panty hoses
She wore a gluey spider web,
Besides, she had a pair of pegs.

A doctor treats my dire neurosis.

Near Midnight

It is already near midnight,
The cozy berth is occupied,
My boat is copulating
With the old screeching dock
While seagulls also mating
Then marching on the rock.

While winds still wrestle
With my rundown vessel,
I looked around just in case
And saw her gorgeous face.

A face of Primavera,
An icon of a goddess,
As if it is another era
Gently descends upon us.

A sad beginning of the end,
Her husband held her hand.
A cherub didn't miss my heart;
It's still in me, that Venus' dart,
So many moons passed by,
I am still whispering goodbye.

My Eyes are Numb

My life is a sinking ship of fools,
Drifting along the blinding lights;
In search of lands without rules
And wisdom of the starry nights.

Under the looming gloom,
I am hiding in a tiny room
Inside the downtown slum
Governed by rule of thumb.

My constant state of melancholy
Looks like a tattered suit I wear,
Only my dog, my border collie,
Brings comfort here and there.

It was not larceny or theft,
I raked the grit of madness
Until there was nothing left,
But just a muted sadness.

My mood's erratic swings
Derive from my inner voices,
I am not a saint without wings,
I simply made a few bad choices.

My rosy dreamy bubbles burst,
Life morphed into the April first.

My Emptiness

My needs have doubled,
But I have less to spend,
No dough, I am troubled,
Oh, well, I wouldn't bend;
I am eating from a trough,
My Lord, don't cut me off.

Life in a rush of daily urges
Absorbing and devastating,
Evocative as ocean surges;
It's over as the lucid grace
Left by a gorgeous face
Of a naked virgin waiting
In ecstasy of her first love;
Push came to shove.
Her first romance is doomed,
The grave of love is tombed.
I can't dislodge my emptiness
After a loss of a new love,
I cannot dodge my edginess
Choked with an iron glove.

I never cross that line
Dividing blood and wine,
I can't rejuvenate
A life approaching death;
I'd rather watch and wait,
I'd rather hold my breath
And reach that final goal
The bond of love and soul.

I Hear My Inner Voice

I hear my inner voice:
''Look in a mirror, you see
A weary stiff marionette,
A shrunken lifeless brie,
A wrinkled old coquette.
Here is your choice:
It's hard to let you go,
It's hard to keep you here.
Just grab your final straw.
Run from your goddamn
Editor and critic-puppeteer.''

I veer between my critic's
Taunting and cruel remarks,
Dodging his verbal blowtorch.
Even the seven rainbow arcs
Don't hide me from the scorch.

I am looking for a gentler slope,
Far from his foggy microscope;
I'll slide into my quiet berth,
Right at the edge of Earth.

But why?
Why do I run like a pimpless
Whore
From the police?
He is a gutless, clueless
Boar,
I am a poet. I am Heracles.

Life is an equation between
A hero and a zero.
I lived as none of the above.

A dumpster fire in a rearview
Mirror
Reminds me of a fuming hate.
I am the other end of this equation.
I've chosen love. Heaven can wait.

Not a Day too Soon

It is so hard to walk
After one learned to fly;
I am an old and lonely hawk,
I'll never touch the sunny sky.

I cannot enter autumn of my days,
I lost my key for its golden room,
A joy of spring and summer's haze,
Will miss the winter's endless gloom.

Without a wish I trace a falling star,
I see my death and close my eyes,
Don't hide; I know who you are,
Come here and put me on the ice.

I played the last chord of my song,
Farewell, my challenging life-tune,
My years were turbulent and long,
I am going out not a day too soon.

I Am Not Insane

Don't temp my uninspiring fate,
Don't stir me with your hate,
Don't chain me with your love,
Your deck is stacked; I bluff.

Chill out, life, give me a hug,
My hands can't hold a mug.

Bartender, you can stop my pain,
Don't let my body croak in vain,
Don't tease my soul and brains,
Decant some rum into my veins.

Don't cure me with your love,
Believe me, I am not insane,
I simply never drink enough;
I only hone my drinking skills
And my sophisticated palette;
My poetry both loves or kills,
It works like stick and carrot.

I am not yet dying from old age,
Those days aren't ready to arrive;
I am trying to evade the cruel edge
Of Damocles' hard-hearted sword
Hanging above my verse's strive…

And I may never pen another word.

I Hear the Drums of War

Despair is near; I hear
The angry drums of war,
They are as insincere
As kisses of a whore.

The songs of our sons
Sung by the fallen stars
After the quiet dawns,
Before the loud guns.

I hate the melody
Of a flying missile,
It irritates my ears.
There is no remedy
When bullets whistle
And tease my fears.

Caress your scars,
They are still sore,
The dice are thrown;
The wars will never end,
Enjoy your girls and bars,
Until we start another war.
The end of wars is known
Only to the dead.

My Dog Was Happy

I am like a one-trick pony
With a self-complacent wit:
After a bowl of fatty macaroni
And drinking chianti quite a bit,
My future doesn't look so grim
Filled with a vodka to the brim.

My dog was timid in the dark
And barked,
My dog was happy as a lark
And barked,
He ran under the rainbow arc
And barked,
I poured a shot of Maker's Mark,
He sang but didn't bark.

I've read in Pavlov's catalogues
That life is simply a dog's whistle
Which shrills like a flying missile;
We act precisely like the dogs:
We bark or bite, we run or hide
And even jumping like the frogs,
Abandoning our bravery behind.

She Was too Beautiful in Lace

Sweet words of a gentle love
Were written on her pretty face,
I made an effort to look tough,
She was too beautiful in lace.

The birds, red as virgin blood
Or ripened cherries in the milk
Enjoyed a supple quilt of snow;
My bride was flaunting lacy silk,
Her passion was a honey flood;
I hope she'll never stop its flow.

Her beaming yet alluring smile
Was like a sunny godsent spell,
Hovering over the church's choir
And leading us to bliss from hell.

My Youth was Strange

My youth was strange,
I learned to break,
I didn't learn to build;
Today, I try to change,
I count every snowflake
Descending on the field.
In total stillness
I watch the nights pass by,
I long for realness,
I truly want to say goodbye.

My finish line is close,
Who needs the words?
The raging streams
Washed friends away,
This dreadful loss
Unlocked the worlds
Unknown to my dreams
Lost in the Milky Way.

I heard the sounds from afar,
I heard the whisper of a star,
"You sold your weary soul,
Counting piece by piece,
You left your father's dome,
You built the tallest wall
And blocked eternal bliss
For those who wait at home."

I sprayed my head
With bits of sparkly gold,
The saints will see
My life more often:
They'll see I am not dead,

I didn't fold, I tried to hold,
I am back, I didn't flee,
I bought myself a coffin,
No ornaments, no brass,
Pure as the crystal glass,
I like the humble graves
Without dates and names.

I hope you hear me, Lord,
Don't hang me out, I am dry,
It's easier done then said;
Give me your solemn word,
That you will never let me die
In my already cold, untidy bed.

My Wisdom Finally Arrived

My wisdom finally arrived,
I signed and broke the mold,
I had a misty, troubled youth,
I killed, I stole, I loved, I lied,
I was afraid, I ran from truth;
Today, I am wise but old.

The vultures circle in the wild,
Descending on my scandals,
I have no time or need to hide
From these repulsive vandals.

Presumption of my innocence
Was burned or ripped to shreds,
My isolation makes no sense,
I am abandoned by my friends.

I used to wear these boots,
I used to wear these hoods,
I just refused to be their prey,
I've seen it all; my hair is grey.

I am holding in my wobbly hands
Addresses in my tatty envelope,
The final bastion of fragile hope,
The sunlit shores of alien lands.

Farewell, my merciless world,
I am off; I dared to cut the cord.

No Wonder We Are Weird

The world of a wicked bedlam
Remembers Eve and Adam,
Their odds were slim to zero,
A god is stronger than a hero,
Instead of mercy or a pardon,
He threw them out of a garden.

The primal family of people
Invented misery and fun,
They faded like a ripple,
Burned with the loving sun.
A first recorded child abuse,
Cain killed a youngster Abel,
And later, we couldn't choose
Between "direct" and "cable".

Then Cain became a father
With seven children,
No women, just his mother,
A sin acutely feared.
Cain lived a life guilt ridden,
No wonder we are weird…

Four lethal horsemen
Have a companion in me,
I am not a dumbstruck lamb,
Neither am I a perfect ten,
I'd hate to pack and flee,
Then drown in the traffic jam.

Life is too short,
Just ask the dead,
Life is a monkey court,
I write a verse instead.

My Body is a Shell

I married such a pretty girl,
A smoothly Southern pearl.
Her room was dark, unknown,
Even a shaky wick was blown.
I chose a timid bourgeois life,
I chose a sulky mindless wife.
A sweet and tender epigraph
Turned into a bitter epitaph.

I surely lost my magic touch,
Her dour nature gains on me,
I hope I am not asking much,
I want her only in my memory.

I am a rooster; I wouldn't give
A damn
Beyond my cock-a-doodle-doo.
I am like a slaughtered lamb,
I am quiet only in the stew.
I won't get out of this life alive,
When all the others sail, I dive.

Dear world of make-believe,
My body is a shell:
Dawn doesn't bring a day,
My heart is empty,
Just rinse me in your sieve
Then serve me on the tray
And I will freeze in hell
Or get the horn of plenty.

My Buddy Vincent

I wrote a card and sent it,
I wished, "Dear Vincent,
Joyeux Noel, Happy New Ear!"
He answered, "Paul, my dear,
Your humor earned a cent,
Let's have absinthe and beer,
Stop by our old saloon,
I'll try to be there soon."
As always, I came first,
Asked for a hefty drink
To clear my convoluted head,
And satisfy my constant thirst.
Van Gogh was on the brink,
Alas he didn't come. Instead,
He went to see a starry night,
Yet had a piece of cheese to bite.

I found a safe haven, a pied-a-terre
In my, I've-seen-this-movie, heart,
A very smart,
Old-fashioned axiomatic laissez-faire
Allowed me to separate his manners
From his art.

My Chances are Too Slim

Sharp as a broken glass,
Abandoned as the last frontier,
It's like a pain in my tight ass,
Wrapped in a petrifying fear;
Death walks into my dreams,
I see her halo brightly gleams.

I asked my angel in the past,
"Don't stop the milky river,
Don't mud the honey dew,
Its bitterness won't last,
Just try; you may deliver
Not only to the chosen few."

My character isn't amended,
I am still loyal to my friends,
I simply burn my candle
From both ends.

My chances are too slim
Above the angry clouds,
Please, pour it to the rim,
Don't justify my doubts.

Wrapped in My Art

New Christmas trees
Determinedly grow
Down from the skies;
I snatched this one
With glossy filigrees.
A fiery sunset's glow
Like cracking ashes
Of our long goodbyes
To the awaited dawn
Out of water splashes.

Only the olden vines
Yield tasty morsels;
I intertwine the lines
To shape my verses.

I painted our town red,
You sensed a déjà vu,
While you were mad,
I paddled **_our_** canoe.

At dawn, I willingly
Laid bare my heart,
I brought you glee
Wrapped in my art.

No Wounds, No Scars

I said goodbye,
Ten days passed by,
You said farewell,
I rang the bell,
I think we split forever,
We're wise, not clever.

Intensely brief,
Love was a tug of war;
Boots on the ground,
Heads in the air,
We were war bound,
We lost the flair,
Please, leave,
Don't shut the door,
Tonight, I want to see
A bunch of falling stars,
No wounds, no scars,
I'll make a wish and flee.

No Past Can be Distilled

No past can be distilled,
No future can be guessed,
Am I half-emptied or half-filled,
In quest for an unknown best?
I seldom hear hello,
I rarely say goodbye,
I meander in this flow
Without knowing why.

A perfect sunny day,
A godsent masterpiece.
You left; you ran away;
A sadly infantile caprice.
Dogs didn't bark, birds didn't fly,
I was demonstrably moonstruck,
I stared into this endless rain,
A livid lightning streaked the sky,
A thunder rolled its heavy truck
Over the merciless hurricane...

Moons vanished, you returned
And gently mumbled, "I am back,
I suffered, bled and learned.
Let's run together our track."
"After your heartless play,
I am lost in unforgiving weeds.
I am waiting for a better day
To sow much kinder seeds."

The wise men trust in change,
The humble trust in status quo,
I am determined to rearrange
The paradigm of Jane and Joe.

This caustic world is ours to lose,
We can't return it to a sender.
Lives ending in a single noose,
Same for a goose or for a gander.

Nights Bury You and Me

A healing balm
Is not invented,
Our stoic calm
Was only rented.

Two helpless daisies,
Two fallen wilted petals,
Two irritated crazies,
Two loud empty kettles.

We lost our desire to talk
About truths and myths,
About failures and ascend;
We lost our desire to walk
Through our spiritual gifts,
Across our life's quicksand.

We fight, we run and fall,
We are against the wall,
Nights bury you and me
In our pursuit of alchemy.

A healing balm
Is not invented,
Our stoic calm
Was only rented.

Necrology

My well forgotten loves,
Climbing the highest pole,
Impatient hawks and doves,
They are fighting for my soul;
I am deft, they are awfully fast,
I won so many battles in the past.

Walkways of nihilism
Meander across the dusty streets
Under infectious air of pessimism,
Fraught with a fruitless promise
Of some absurdly sugared treats
But I am a sceptic, not a novice.

I lived with blinding shine of gold,
I live with soiled misery of copper,
I boldly played and have been fold,
At night, I'll fail to pull a rabbit
From my empty coffer.

My soul is washed and aired,
My aptitude is totally impaired,
I cannot write a decent verse
Without anguish or a laughter:
My gears stock in reverse
Before and during, even after.

I threw away my iron gloves
And wrote a letter to my loves:
I sent my most sincere apology
To those who knew
Cuffed wrists and chained legs,
To those who knew the noose.
I finished writing my necrology,

And hocked the priceless goose
Delivering these golden eggs.

I didn't have a wink of sleep,
I am not ready for my buddies'
Parting weep,
I am not ready for a spineless
Unexciting bliss,
I am not ready for a single day
Without a kiss.

Never Chosen

The furniture is changed,
The photos rearranged,
My dusty windows-eyes
Are covered with the ice.

She reached her goal,
No more a stranger,
She moved into my soul,
No more an angel.

I walk over the edge,
It's forced upon me,
I am never chosen;
Along the parody of life,
I run away from glee
Which is untimely frozen.

I stand under the wedges
Of flying regal cranes;
They look like arrowheads
Of our Southern lives
Retelling our ancient affairs
With rather blurry images
Of worthless midnight divas,
Who entertain the heirs
Of ineffective old ideas.

A man will not forgive
If treated with contempt,
He may abruptly leave
If asked to be exempt.

Saint Peter Gulped a Pint

I walk between two lines,
I didn't write them straight,
They interweave two vines
Of love and hate...

The morsels of my weary mind,
The fruits of sleepless nights,
Can't help. I am lost, I cannot find
My life's inspiring sights...

I couldn't avoid the deep pitfalls
Of my paranoid fear of scores,
They're left by hefty cannonballs
From ancient devastating wars...

My verdict was delivered by eleven,
Someone escorted Judas outdoors.

Saint Peter gulped a pint,
Then shut the Holy gate,
"Keep off!" he sighed.
I learned my ordinary fate...

Its Final Destination

In wake of uninvited death,
I calmly wished good day
To dawn's fresh breath.
Sunrise was on the way.

The river streams again,
Seeps through the siege,
And drowns like insane
Under the ancient bridge.
A guiltless natural farewell
To a nasty, bad-luck raven,
Revisiting a stone-cold hell,
Reentering his frozen haven.

When reason sleeps,
My wisdom sadly sighs;
A bright tomorrow leaps
Into the timid sea of lies,
Into a willful devastation,
Into its final destination.

If I could have a mirrored wall,
It would reflect my downfall
Under the innocence of stars,
Between the prison's bars.

It is extremely quiet in the eyes
Of godsent cruel hurricanes;
My soul escaped into the skies,
It failed to outlive my body pains.

The Leaves are Fully Turned

The blinding kindness,
The darkness of a ploy,
The weight of lightness,
The sadness of a joy.

The leaves are fully turned,
The winter pushes our door,
The lessons are not learned,
The shadows slash the floor.

Look at the amazing sight,
Look up and see the stars,
Look at the naughty Mars,
Look at the morning light.

We will survive a rainy weather,
We do not live by bread alone,
We are alive and still together,
We reap what we have sown.

The Leo Sign

Zeus rearranged the Zodiac design,
I was created under the Leo sign,
Right after me Zeus broke the mold,
This is, at least, what I was told.

All Leos are the birdies of a feather:
Pay no attention to the weather,
Lie on the beach while it is snowing,
Wear furs while our sun is glowing.

We see the sign "Use Caution",
But put our energies in motion,
We press our hammers down
To the highest gears,
We are involved in every race
Just to enjoy the cheers.

We know thorns from petals
Even through rose-colored glasses,
We are the fish from other kettles
Unknown to the common masses.

Those who were born in August
Can see the truth under the dust,
At times, we are the joyous "haves",
You hear our sparkling toxic laughs,
At times, we are the poor "have-nots"
And solemnly connect the dots.
We do not live by bread alone,
This universe is our comfort zone.

The Loveless Hell

The gold of maples,
The blues of our skies
Descended on my mind;
The ploys and fables,
The bitterness of lies
Ascended to the blind.

My friends have gone,
Only their photos last
To face another dawn.
We lived in our past,
It was not good enough
To save our fragile love.

The pain of our farewell
Was hidden in the bags;
The burning chill of hell
Turn riches into the rags.

Two gray Canadian swans
Saw only black and white,
Enjoyed the early dawns,
But didn't see the daily light.

Sad loneliness and grief
Paved our pathetic path
Toward the endless well;
The suffering of our days
Wasted on hopeless plays
Has outlived the loveless hell.

The Magic Flute

We pay a hefty price
For our dreamy eyes,
For our teary clouds;
We are the hounds
Forever in pursuit
Of the evasive loot.

The ship of fools
Unfurls its sails:
We close our school,
We open our jails.
No smoke, no flame,
No one to blame,
Forever in pursuit
Of the evasive loot.

We combed a distant land,
We sadly swung between
Our victories and losses;
There is no helping hand,
We were not asked,
"Where have you been?
What have you seen?"
As if we hide or masked,
As if we are as wild
As friendless albatrosses.

Neglected perils
Defeated our barrels,
And ended our game;
We never had a real aim,
We ended our vain pursuit,
Misguided by the magic flute.

The Melting Shawl of Winter

Old winter being death bound,
Unchained the naked trees,
And let the sun to fool around,
And let Icicles drop their tears.

The melting shawl of winter
Still hides the shores of life,
I am a south bound sprinter,
I run into my Dixie to survive.

I love the Southern starry night,
The moon above coyotes' howl,
The dinners with a candlelight,
And our drawl in every vowel.

I dive into my Southern life,
I swim in its caressing lightness,
I wish to meet a Southern wife,
The lovely cradle of politeness.

The dire and vicious Civil War
Left us with wounds and scars,
We learned to live, keep score,
And laugh under the fifty stars.

The good old boys and gents
Have learned to meet the ends;
We live off our abundant lands,
With our wives and our girlfriends.

The Milk is Spilled

The milk is spilled,
It is too late to cry,
And wash our guilt
Under the rainy sky.

A visit to a judge was brief,
The final word is still afloat,
It is our love's fallen leaf
It is our love's sinking boat.

We didn't reach the truce,
Totally exhausted, starved,
We killed the golden goose,
Tonight, it will be carved.

We drag a heavy bag
Of our faded dreams,
And even a glossy tag
Is numb or so it seems.

We walk,
The wintry air gets colder,
We talk,
A furry river of your mink
Runs from your shoulder,
Streams down a full link.

The well of love is dry,
We check it every day,
Nobody wants to cry,
Nobody wants to pay.

Moonlight is Sliding into My Room

Moonlight is sliding into my room
Through old and careless shutters,
It is a restless night, I am a groom,
I even hear my bride still mutters.

My loud, thumping heart
Echoes the church's bell,
This night we sleep apart,
We are escaping hell.

Today, love and old rules collide,
Tomorrow, I will see my bride,
Tomorrow, I will enjoy a life,
Tomorrow, I will have a wife.

The dreams and hopes
Swirl in my wobbly soul,
I am a boxer on the ropes,
An actor who forgot his role.

I know love, I see its end,
My patience will run thin,
I will compromise and bend,
I will wind up in a highway inn.

The lawyers skim the milk,
Display a very happy grin,
Wrap every case with silk,
We lose, they always win.

The Music Flew Away

The songs of our day,
The symphonies of life,
All of a sudden flew away
Hence silence must arrive.

I turned the globe,
I hoped to find bliss,
It was a quixotic probe
Of my illusions in a breeze.

Your mink coat streamed
From shoulders to the floor,
You stood and gleamed,
A real goddess at the door.

The sunbeams bounce
Off the perfect oval of your face;
I wish to be one of those clowns
Descending just to see your grace.

Again, you've gone somewhere,
I can no longer keep the score,
You simply vanished from my glare,
And left only a shadow on the floor.

Another drama,
Farewell, my friend,
Another trauma,
The same old trend.

I gloomily do it right
Through many years,
I cry only at night,
Nobody sees my tears.

The Moon Intoned a Lullaby

The moon intoned a lullaby,
At last, I am entirely free,
The stars blink me goodbye,
I drift over a dreamy sea.

I live another hopeful day,
I shake a tin cup of a beggar,
I lost the battle anyway,
I am on my knee and beg her.

I hold my muse's tender arm,
She lifts me from my knees,
I didn't write, there is no harm,
I smile and she forgives.

The merciless rude alarm
Brakes silence of my dreams,
In spite of a gallant charm
Reality is awful as it seems.

The moon is a coin flipped,
Sings her soothing lullaby,
I write a happy, witty script,
My muse waves her goodbye.

The Malachite of Grass

The malachite of grass
Was our bed and shrine,
That day, I filled my glass
With tender love, not wine.

If happiness could grow
On a tree,
I would become a forest
Ranger,
I'd walk across a verdant
Glee,
As wisemen to the manger.

We parted ways,
Reality is cruel
As an iron glove,
Within its craze
I am still in love;
That glass is full.

I desperately looked for you
From sunshine to moonlight;
I saw the diamonds of dew
As tears of a mourning night.

I learned that all must pass,
Today, I drank that glass.
Love had to face its death,
I've heard its final breath.

The Master Keys

A gypsy found on my palm
Two troubled lines of glee,
I took it with a grain of salt,
I couldn't win a Grand Prix,
I couldn't break the vault.

I shut the windows of my soul,
No one will ever look inside,
I'd rather lose the title role,
Then crawl away and hide.

Remorse didn't convince my saints,
Confession fell on angels' idle ears.
The teary rains washed off my sins,
These days, I learn to curb my fears.

I locked the doors,
No one can forge,
No one can falsify
The master keys.
I will not ever fly
Above the gorge,
Or naked trees.
I will just glitter
Out of my corner.
As if I am from Jupiter
As if I am a foreigner.

I curbed my outrage:
The plodding dinosaurs
Or even flying raptors
Under their masks,
Behind the doors,
Don't ever leave the stage,
They are eternal actors.

Youth Was a One-Night Stand

Youth was just a one-night stand.
I meandered from the primal day
In labyrinths of yet unknown land,
While years painted my hair gray.

The powerholders of those days
Marched in their muddy boots
Through my integrity and grace
Straight to my yet fragile roots.

My destiny was built on sand,
I walked and ran on feet of clay,
My victories were seldom planned.
I only scored my failures every day.

Please, hear my anxious groans
And comprehend their meaning,
Milestones became tombstones
While red sunsets were gleaming.

My hopes ascended into bliss,
Returned as flowers of spring,
As innocence of a baby's kiss,
As tunes the birds forever sing.

At night, when the darkness falls
My memories cast shadows
On the walls,
And only my ever-trembling hand
Reminds me that my youth
Was just a one-night stand.

The Night Fell on Saint Mark

It is my last Venetian sight:
The night fell on Saint Mark,
Your gondola's inviting light
Gleams lonely in the dark.

So bright and loud is the night,
Even the seagulls wouldn't fly,
Gray pigeons stopped to fight
As if their anger said goodbye.

I drown in a comfortable chair
And sip my brandy with a flair,
I hunt the most imaginative costumes,
And smell marijuana's dreamy fumes.

I like those wicked, enigmatic nights
When even a sinner wears the whites,
When golden masks veil dark desires
Until the ancient masquerade expires.

The boats turn off their merry motors,
The ripples hint their pointless goals,
The stars rock in the muddy waters,
I trail the silhouettes of dancing souls.

I camouflage my fears in shiny smiles,
I hide my sins in teardrops of my eyes.

It is my last Venetian sight,
The night fell on Saint Mark,
Your gondola's inviting light
Gleams lonely in the dark.

The Noose of Years

The noose of years
Held back the clock,
I changed the sticky gears,
And heard tick-tock, tick-tock.

Good-looking gondoliers
Kick walls of ancient villas
And fork the muddy tides,
I see the busy sommeliers
Flirting with the aging divas
And rival with the other guides.

I sensed a shade of menace
Under the guise of love,
An unexpected pleasant call:
"It is my final night in Venice;
I am an angel from above,
From heaven wall-to-wall,
Good morning, dear,
I'd like to see you, I am near."

"Please, come," I said, "I am game";
She quickly came,
I saw a tall and wingless angel
Straight ahead:
A gorgeous, splendid stranger
Much tastier than a slice of bread,
Much sweeter than a French éclair,
More needed than a book I've read,
And surely better than my last affair.

The tale is silver,
The truth is gold,
Van Gogh cut off his ear
Because his bed was cold.

The Numbered Days

The numbered days
Of our lives on Earth
Selecting our ways
To death from birth.

I am sitting on my hands,
I am asked to be discreet,
I am gaining futile friends,
I am agonizing in defeat.

It is a life without freedom
My long and starless night;
While heaven is still hidden
Beyond my full-fledged flight.

Life is a never-ending freeze,
Life is a slaughterhouse,
No lights, no doors, no keys;
I hide amid the naked trees
As if I am the second mouse
That always gets the cheese.

The Tango of Two Broken Hearts

I asked to fix a hefty drink,
A skilled bartender poured,
And gave me his ironic wink.
The tango hit another chord…

We are one; our shadows dance
The tango of two broken hearts,
Away from Cupid's gentle glance
And whistles of his missing darts.

The tango of two broken hearts
Stirred memories we fondly kept;
Our feet imprinted fancy charts,
We laughed; yet our souls wept.
The tango was a soothing balm,
The shadows gracefully swayed,
Our embrace was tight and calm,
Yet our love was doomed to fade.

The skies were waiting
For the sun to rise
Amid the choking nightly
Southern heat,
But suddenly, a bolt of
Lightning
Threw its cracking dice.
The raindrops set the beat,
Pinning the dust
Into the thirsty dancing floor.

Your face betrays it all,
There is no sign of love;
You dance over my soul,
I call your heartless bluff.

Please, stop,
Don't pirouette me
To the end of our loves.
Restart the tango from the top,
Let's hold our fate and glee
In our tender gloves.

The rain will go away,
Bandoneons will play.

Alone

I watched the bright hostile sunrise,
I couldn't cast a shadow on the floor;
I watched with reprimanding eyes,
I couldn't thread a needle anymore,
I couldn't cast a shadow on the floor.

I failed to pay attention
To the canaries in the mines.
I was a bone of that contention;
I crossed the sacramental lines.
I dashed on my worn-out horse
Back to my miserable failure;
I am expecting genuine remorse
From a sadistic, merciless jailer.

These days, I run my track
Without ever looking back.
I am waiting in the wings
To buy a place in paradise;
My acquiescent angel-muse
Pulls all the known strings
To get a dirt-cheap price
For rooms with better views.

Suddenly, I am left alone
Without foes and friends.
My epitaph was carved in stone
Before my tatty soul ascends:
"We laid him on a Petri dish,
He lived as a sagacious man
Without any doubts in his wish,
He never had a masterplan."

Gray Silhouettes of Friends

Gray silhouettes of friends
Quietly stroll before my eyes
Like our old fashioned trends,
Like tiny birds up in the skies,
Like shadows from mirages,
Like innocence abandoned
In bloody battles for survival,
Like pieces of cubist collages
That unintentionally landed
On pages of the Holy Bible.

It surely comes as no surprise,
Nobody wears a cheerful attire
In spiderwebs of old quagmires.
Nothing is new under the sun,
When life turns perilous or dire,
A few may fight, the others run.

We seek the power of fame,
The perfect crimes
Or just a perfect game.
Why most of us, at times,
Believe in love?
We never have been helped
By those who fly above.

The countdown has begun.
Don't try to answer, not today,
When angels help at dawn,
At dusk you will be asked to pay.
A borrower is just a lackey
Of a lender;
Try not to take, return to sender.

I Want So Much

I want so much,
I want to be in touch
With all that passes
My thorny, stirring life.

At noon, I am a go-getter;
At night, I am a city tramp.
I am a never opened letter;
I am a pothole on the ramp;
I didn't become much better
After I rubbed Aladdin lamp.

Cacophony of fragments,
Hostilities of ugly creases,
Disasters from the start;
When my intuition's dragnets
Rake all the worthy pieces,
Life morphs into a work of art:
Into cacophony of fragments,
Into hostilities of ugly creases,
And problems from the start.

I tried to be a decent man,
I learned to love and hate,
At times, I crawled or ran
Toward the promised gate.

Life rolls its luring waters;
In vain, I throw in my shily quarters;
In vain, I disregard a wise advice,
I try to enter the same river twice.

Odds and Ends

Unfortunately, life disappears
Into the sea of tears and cheers;
Even my relatives and friends
Cease to exist as odds and ends.

Life is still dangerous and fast;
I can no longer catch my breath.
Today, I am running from my past;
At night, I may entertain my death.

I heal my difficulties' roots,
A doctor cures his patients,
While life gifts pointless fruits
And overstated expectations.

I regularly moan or cry
Over my buddies' graves;
I heard their souls don't fly,
But float over the quiet waves.

At times, death stares at me,
And rather eloquently winks.
I am a sailor, I wouldn't flee,
I stand like the regal sphynx.

Rain varnished cobblestones
Of my dilapidated ancient road,
Flanked by remortgaged homes
With an objectionable zip code.

My Bucket List

I imitated a pace car,
Ahead of everybody for a while;
But truly, I am just a fallen star,
And am still waiting for the trial.

The obelisk of truth collapsed,
And I am buried underneath;
The ancient axioms of youth
Deteriorated and elapsed,
Yet I am fighting nails and teeth.

Only the law and reasons
Stop at the doors of prisons.
My mind stops at the doors
Of wishful thinking and illusions;
I like my doubts and confusions.

I rarely am a host or guest
Of tales and myths well-known,
I am rather in the quest
Of Zeus' unfortunate desire:
I am old Prometheus
Who is again so cruelly thrown
To rediscover secrets of the fire.

I am not yet a snowflake
That fell into the melting snow.
Even the nature needs a brake
To readjust this endless flow.

The lilac's aromatic cluster
Ignores my ego and conniption;
It flaunts its blinding luster
As basic commonality
To godly stubborn fiction
And our gullible reality.

My bucket list
Is not determined yet;
I seldom shout, often twist,
I never win, but always bet.

From Dusk to Dawn

We see much better in the dark,
As owls we hunt our prey at night,
Even those pairs from Noah's Ark,
Most likely, hunted for a juicy bite.

I am sure God meanders in the skies,
I guess He doesn't want to find us;
Who pulls the wool over our eyes
Then dumps us under a moving bus?

Only from dusk to dawn
My crazy life still goes on.
At dawn, I asked the Lord,
"We only dream of heaven,
While living in our daily hell.
Why only your son soared,
But each of ours just fell?"

He said," I wished to drop a gavel
On people's scandalous discords,
But sins were stacked too high;
I buried some but braked a shovel
Then cut your planet's primal cord
And waved your sons goodbye.
Today, I penciled in my journal:
Your troubles seem to be eternal."

A man still has the seventh day
To generate the world unknown.
Our future is already on the way.
The dice was resolutely thrown.

.

Graffiti

Please, take a shower.
It's not a time for glory;
Don't throw in the towel,
I am here to tell the story.

The rite of spring:
I walk still fresh and tall,
The birds don't sing;
I read graffiti on the wall,
"Unjustly written law
Is not my law,
At all!
Not every problem
Is a nail,
Not every solution
Is a hammer!
We fail to trust,
We choose to bail,
A jail is not a must,
Unlock the slammer!
The jailed birds never sing
Even for the rite of spring."

The Poets Can't Imagine

What is the world without wars?
Why do we trust those very few
Who never look under the hoods?
I wonder if they ever left the woods.
Even my Pegasus, a literary horse
Appreciates the churches' whores,
But can't believe in something new.

I'll help you to recall
How the peace began:
The fires over Saigon,
The bullet ridden wall,
They marched; we ran;
Those days have gone.

I healed my gloom,
I bit the silver bullet,
I left that cozy womb,
I had the guts to do it.

Even the poets can't imagine
How the mental illness ends,
The Big Bang is not an engine
Among the modern trends.

I am running my own track,
Don't ask where I am from;
I want to go back,
I want to go home.

The Pine Trees Grow

The pine trees grow,
The winds caress the sand,
The lazy clouds flow,
We walk, I hold your hand.

I don't regret the past,
It was a university of life,
I kept black powder dry;
I am alive and free at last
To teach my hopes to fly
Above our eternal strife.

I am tired of this strive,
I need only a day of rest
While I am still alive.
I am sworn to do my best.

The sun still glows
The time still flows.
I had a day of rest…

The Specter of Schooldays

His image regularly lingers,
The specter of schooldays:
Arthritic domineering fingers,
And malice of a spider's face.

He was a filthy moralist,
He was a pervert priest,
The bible bashing nihilist,
First on the devil's list.

Some men live in denial,
Some women in delusion,
Some people seek a trial,
Some just endure confusion.

I ride one of the wooden horses
Of my life's ceaseless carousel;
I missed some tasty morsels,
But passed the gates of hell.

I hate the spine-chilling sleaze
Of our faiths' houses of cards;
I am afraid the hell may freeze
Before we change the guards.

The Road Less Traveled

I hit the road less traveled,
Still clueless in this region,
My guide was left behind,
I am entirely unraveled;
Even a common pigeon
Deserves a better mind.

I changed my stripes
And jumped into a pit,
It is too cold;
The pressure wipes
My deprecating wit,
I am too old.

Only the fallen angels
Don't know when to fold;
A well-baked vengeance
Is better to serve cold.

I think it is my time to fold,
I am eighty-four tonight.
Is this infinity's threshold
Or the dawn of a new fight?

I am ready for the snow,
Farewell, my cozy rainy fall,
When rivers stop their flow,
Cold winters warm my soul.

The Old Man's Jolly Fest

I sing to lull the dread
In every willing bar,
Across the winter's frost,
No sun above my head;
The strings of my guitar
Saved every song I lost.

Girls love me when I sing
I almost rob the cradles;
Here comes another spring,
The sun hangs on the gables,
I park my car, open the door,
She smiles;, I love her more.

A silky dress naughtily clings
To her long legs and chest,
She is my angel with two wings;
She is this old man's jolly fest.

Two lonely souls,
Damaged by life
Of arguments and brawls,
We truly straggled to survive.
There's no novel in her eyes,
Only a short but lovely story,
No issue for a compromise,
Just a straight path to glory.

The leaves fall off the tree,
Two lovers sailing as two boats
Without a compass in the sea,
Without maps and even notes.

I often meet these fallen angels,
Yet never use a sweet corruption,

Only a willingness of strangers,
And innocence of introduction.

I never use the calendar of fears,
A day of laughs, a night of tears;
I rather open the Pandora's chest,
The old man's jolly fest...

The Sea Makes Love to Earth

The sea makes love to earth,
I watch, I am not a showboat,
I am still anchored to my berth,
I have survived and stay afloat.

Abundant shores of youth,
I am your disobedient son,
I have returned to learn the truth
Before the memories have gone.

The scent of a baked bread,
Sweet as my mother's lullaby,
Brought by a grey-haired friend,
A symbol of the time passed by.

During the rainy days
The spongy clouds cry,
They hide the sunny rays
In quiet dungeons of the sky.

The rods of lightning
Fork through the hails,
The winds still fighting
And feed the hungry sails.

The boats rock on the waves,
The seagulls face the wind,
A flagpole bends and sways,
Looks like a boy who sinned.

I keep my powder dry,
Tomorrow, I will sail
Into the endless sky,
To see the Holy Grail.

The Show is Over

Life is not a tenacious book,
We do not read its final page:
The Greco-Roman fables,
The faded nations' morsels,
Gods fly above the gables,
Olympian almighty torsos
Abduct the Sabine women
To share their noble semen.

Zeus wouldn't wait or beg,
He fell for Leda as a swan,
She laid the godsent egg,
The show tried to go on.

Dejected actors left
Deprived and sober,
No strings attached;
The rainbow arched
To beautify the theft.
The showbiz is over.

Don't weep, my friend,
Don't close your eyes,
Just shake my hand,
Enjoy your last sunrise.

Our old certificate of birth
Is our certificate of death,
Farewell, our beloved Earth,
Don't even hold your breath.

The show ceased its season,
We are silent on the gloomy stage,
The book of life defined the reason,
But we refused to read its final page.

The Falling Petals

The tasteless rap
Bombards my head,
The cacophonic crap
Turns city streetlights red.

The falling petals of red roses
Cover the footprints on my trails;
My pain, after the doorway closes,
Erases memories of small details.

I breathe through sad delusions
Disguised by decorated fabrics,
As rather cheerful confusions
Of hooligans and mavericks.

The days are passing by,
My lifelong train derails,
Soon, I will say goodbye
To centuries old tales.

Four Seasons

I noosed too many ropes,
I used a vicious guillotine,
A labor of love and hatred,
No accidents in any cases.
I buried a few dying hopes,
Some virtues, never a sin.
A public moral deafness
Was silently created,
But our good and evil
Kept their poker faces.

I am working as a hired butcher,
I am neither a predator nor prey,
I never think about our future:
I fight, survive and walk away.

This constant spring must end
Then summer will descend
To rule awhile this nutty globe,
Then fall will get a golden robe.
And winter with the rest of us
Who dream of entering the sky,
Will end the day under the bus
Trying to eat and flaunt the pie.

I am waiting at the end
Of a lifelong angry line,
Holding the end of a rope.
A life is not a daily trend;
My life is a fragile twine
That pulls a foggy hope.

You Hold a Password to My Heart

The sun is carefully rising,
There is a sail on the horizon,
It is my drifting, lonely soul
In quest of an unknown goal.

The ripples flaunt white lace,
My boat rocks on the waves,
Moves like an aimless swan,
Embraced by the grace of sun.

You hold a password to my heart,
But I am not familiar with the art
Of a daily jealousy without guides,
And bitter whispers of the tides
About the shocking breezes
After the sunny mornings,
About silent warnings
Before love freezes.

I changed a password to my heart,
Don't try to break my crystal dream,
Be careful, don't push too hard,
Don't put a dam across the stream.

Today, I learned to walk

I flew like a cascade
Over the prison wall,
I fly, that's what I want to do,
I'm illicitly a red tailed hawk,
Don't ever ruin my charade,
I fly as an uprising waterfall,
I fly, that's what I always do,
I fly; I'll never crawl or walk.

Queen's "let them eat cake"
To "les miserable" have-nots,
They stormed the old Bastille,
Nobody vowed in the wake
Damn chickens in their pots
Or even a half decent meal.

Don't promise anything,
Cease rivers of your money,
Cling to your lighting dash,
Remember, you're not a king,
Just sip your milk-and-honey,
Enjoy your lovers' flash.

My lies become too friendly,
My dreams take me away,
I'll leave the horn of plenty,
Among mirages of today.

I am on the way to Guatemala,
I like Antigua's rums and coffees,
I listen to the Ninth of Mahler
It soars over the ancient coffins.

I'm bored,
The same horrific carnage,
No news under the moon,
My lord,
Get some real knowledge
From these natives, soon.

I am a wingless hawk,
Today, I learned to walk,
One basket for all eggs
Until my final breath,
I am walking on my pegs,
I try to outsmart my death.

The Spears of Avenues

Diagonally wandering Broadway
Crawls over the concrete jungle,
The arrows of the streets at play,
The old New York looks younger.

Fast as the daily news
We run across the park,
Like spears of avenues
Under the rainbow arc.

My scruffy yellow taxi runs
Like a downhearted bride;
The famous restaurants
Invite me with a lurid pride.

I've seen the moons
Walked out on the nights,
I outlived those swoons,
I simply won some fights.

I am scarred and wind-burned
Faced,
I am a walking diary of our dire
Wars:
We lived a life, my friends and I
Embraced,
Today, I am the one who keeps
Those jolly scores.

I am in New York alone,
Forsaken in the fairyland;
I am ushered by my phone
Along a redline in the sand.

The Sailors' Wings

The sunken submarine,
The worthless periscope,
Who is that god who let
Young sailors with no sin
To die without hope.

I stride the shaking pier,
I hear their chilling cries;
The bloody sun will rise,
The tears will disappear.

A sunset learns to bleed,
The memories are fading,
I walk across their sighs
Beneath my weary feet,
The paradise is waiting
For comforting goodbyes,

An angel solved the riddle,
The sailors grew the wings,
I play the trembling strings,
They hear my crying fiddle.

The Pain of a Reward

My Pegasus, my horse
Fell from the tractor,
I've seen much worse,
But called a doctor;
He was a dentist's help,
"Don't cry and yelp,
While she can breathe
I'll simply pull her teeth."

That wasn't worth
The pain of a reward,
In heaven or on earth,
Her mother cut the cord.

She used to walk,
She used to fly,
She had two wings,
I know, she'll croak,
At times she'd cry,
Tonight, she sings.

It was an awful curse,
My neck is in the noose,
My poor winged horse
Still is my loving muse,
At times I write a verse,
But mostly sing the blues.

My Pegasus, my horse
Fell from the tractor,
I called a nurse,
I got a goddamn doctor.

Royal Flush

The graveyards of tomorrows
Invite the doubtful and sick;
The boneyards of my sorrows
Persuade the life clocks tick.

We played after we met
A smoothly sweet accord,
Without ever getting wet,
Without going overboard.

You were an actress,
Orgasms were faked,
I rocked the mattress,
You were already baked.

I clearly know the prize:
Let's leave our burrows,
Let's stop our futile cries,
Tears only dig the furrows.

You cut the deck of cards,
I dealt the suite of hearts,
You've got a Royal Flush,
It's yours to win or crush.

One mouse got the cheese;
There were two hungry mice,
Don't guess, don't ever tease,
Enjoy the truth and roll the dice.

A Petrarchan Sonnet

A vicious moth has eaten holes in my tuxedo,
These days, I can't afford to mend my suits,
These days, I deal with my diminishing libido,
My money left me through the chimney flutes.
I miss the hippie days of our psychedelic past,
I didn't like Chopin and kept him in the locker,
When quiet hours would never move too fast,
I loved The Beatles, Hendrix and Joe Cocker.

I thought it was a new Big Bang
When Eric Carmen fondly sang:
"And making love was just for fun,
Those days have gone..."
The melody of life has no refrain,
No words, only the strings of rain

The Spark of Hope

I am your shadow,
You walk, I follow you,
Don't say so long,
I am a bird, a swallow,
I am a song
That is forever new.

I pushed away my muse,
The one I fondly cherished;
I hardly have any excuse,
I think my senses perished.

I run the marathon of time,
Of never-ending thoughts,
I am an arrhythmic chime,
I disconnect the futile dots.

The Justice is not blind,
She is the heaven's dawn,
She is a harbor of my mind,
She is our brightest paragon.

I am an angel with a sword,
Kind to a foe and to a friend;
I am a guardian of our world
Unswerving to the bitter end.

I rarely lose but often gain,
Rejoice, don't ever mourn,
Under the strands of rain
The spark of hope is born.

EPILOGUE

We are those naked lonely trees:
The sky is our blanket.

Acknowledgments

I am deeply and endlessly grateful to Judith Broadbent for her skilled professional guldens and generous stewardship; for her unyielding yet wise editing which gave me enough room to exercise my whims.

To Anna Dikalova for her kind ideas and a firm belief In my success.

To a great artist, Mary Anne Capeci, who allowed me to use her painting for the cover of this book.

To all my friends for their continuous and gently Expressed motivations.

Thanks, y'all.

Printed in the United States
By Bookmasters